THE PARTICIPLE IN THE BOOK OF ACTS

A DISSERTATION

SUBMITTED TO THE FACULTY OF THE GRADUATE DIVINITY SCHOOL
IN CANDIDACY FOR THE DEGREE OF
DOCTOR OF PHILOSOPHY

(DEPARTMENT OF BIBLICAL GREEK)

BY

CHARLES BRAY WILLIAMS

WIPF & STOCK · Eugene, Oregon

Wipf and Stock Publishers
199 W 8th Ave, Suite 3
Eugene, OR 97401

The Participle in the Book of Acts
By Williams, Charles Bray
ISBN 13: 978-1-60608-354-3
Publication date 12/05/2008
Previously published by University of Chicago Press, 1909

Acknowledgment is due to Professors Ernest D. Burton, Clyde W. Votaw, and Edgar J. Goodspeed for their valuable suggestions and criticisms.

CONTENTS

INTRODUCTION

A casual reading impresses the Greek student with the great number and striking variety of participles in the Book of Acts. A critical reading reveals many facts of importance to the New Testament grammarian and theologian. To ascertain these facts and to determine their bearing on the main problems connected with the Book of Acts is the purpose of this treatise.

The WH text is the basis of our investigations. Where this text is in doubt about the reading we shall indicate it, if it bears on the use of the participle. If weighty MSS favor another reading than WH we shall mention it.

PART I

FACTS CONCERNING THE PARTICIPLE IN THE BOOK OF ACTS

CHAPTER I

THE CATEGORIES OF THE PARTICIPLE

Before we can deal intelligently with the participles in Acts we must decide on some principles of classification and adopt a definite classification and terminology for our use in this treatise. The categories of some leading Greek grammarians will first be examined.

SEC. 1. KUEHNER'S CLASSIFICATION

I. Complementary participles used with verbs of perceiving, showing, expressing the emotions, of enduring, beginning, continuing, ceasing, ἔχω, τυγχάνω, λανθάνω, etc.

II. Attributive, expressing an attributive qualification of substantives requiring (in English) a participle after the substantive, or equivalent to a relative clause.

III. Participles used to express adverbial qualification of the principal action.

SEC. 2. GOODWIN'S CLASSIFICATION

I. Attributive. Here he distinguishes the use of the participle as attributive adjective, as substantive (usually with the article), and as predicate adjective.

II. Circumstantial, expressing time, means, manner, cause, condition, concession, etc.

III. Supplementary—not in indirect discourse and also in indirect discourse.

SEC. 3. BURTON'S CLASSIFICATION

I. The adjective participle—attributive and predicative.

II. The adverbial, equivalent to clauses of time, cause, condition, concession, etc.

III. The substantive, used as part of subject, object, or limiting genitive. This class corresponds to Goodwin's supplementary class.

I

SEC. 4. JANNARIS' CLASSIFICATION

He says there are two general uses and so two general classes:

I. The adjectival participle, divided into the attributive which is often equivalent to a relative clause, and the predicative participle which like a predicate "supplements the notion of certain incomplete or auxiliary verbs." The latter is the supplementary class of Kuehner and Goodwin, the substantive class of Burton.

II. The adverbial participle, expressing time, cause, condition, concession, etc.

SEC. 5. WINER'S CLASSIFICATION

He did not give any definite classification, but speaks of:

I. Participles expressing a complement to a principal sentence and illustrates this class with ἀπῆλθεν λυπούμενος, which is almost surely an adverbial participle of manner.

II. Participles expressing subordinate 'sentences, illustrating this class with πᾶν κλῆμα μὴ φέρον and μένον σοὶ ἔμενεν, one of which examples is attributive and the other adverbial (according to the terminology of Kuehner, Goodwin, and Burton).

III. Participles used as a complement, or predicatively, illustrating this class with ἐπέμενε κρούων, etc. His first two classes are not exclusive and hence his classification is not logical.

SEC. 6. BLASS'S CLASSIFICATION

He makes only two classes:

I. Participles as attributive. But he makes this class include the attributive and supplementary of Goodwin.

II. Participles expressing an additional clause, corresponding to the adverbial or circumstantial class of Goodwin or Burton.

SEC. 7. HADLEY AND ALLEN'S CLASSIFICATION

I. Attributive, the participle often being substantive as well as adjectival.

II. Predicate-participles divided into the subclasses:

1. Circumstantial, expressing time, means, manner, cause, etc.

2. Supplementary.

Babbitt, who had begun his Greek grammar in partnership with Allen before the latter's death, follows, not Hadley and Allen's, but Goodwin's, classification.

Sec. 8. Delbrück-Brugmann's Classification

They discuss, but not with unreserved approval, Classen's classification:

I. The participle of external relation.

II. The adverbial participle.

III. The objective participle.

They make the "time-character" of the participle the basis of division, but surely the time element in the participle does not furnish the best basis of classification.

Sec. 9. Viteau's Classification

Viteau does not show the relation of the great classes of the participle, but merely discusses twelve subclasses: The participle of distinctive complement (used with the article to characterize a person or thing); the participle of attributive complement (used without the article to denote the quality or manner of being or transient action); the explicative participle (equivalent to a relative proposition); the final participle (purpose and consequence); the causal; the conditional and concessive; the temporal; the attributive with particles; the periphrastic; the attributive connected with the subject (with τυγχάνω, παύομαι, etc.); attributive connected with the object (with verbs of seeing, knowing, etc.); the independent participle (genitive, accusative, and nominative absolute).

Sec. 10. Some General Criticisms on These Categories

We must not stop to go too far into details, and yet we must make some criticism on these classifications.

First, there seems to be naturally a threefold classification of Greek participles, as is recognized by Kuehner, Goodwin, Burton, Babbitt, Classen, etc.   It scarcely seems logical to throw together the first and third classes, as did Blass and Jannaris, nor is it any more natural to combine the second and third classes, as did Hadley and Allen.   The participle illustrated by πόλις οἰκουμένη is different in nature from that in ἐλθὼν εἶδον, and it seems equally as different in function from that in the sentence ὁράω αὐτὸν ἐρχόμενον.   In the first example the function of the participle is to ascribe a state, and so a characteristic, to πόλις, just as καλή would do in πόλις καλή.   In the second example ἐλθὼν clearly takes the place of a subordinate clause and modifies the action of εἶδον, while ἐρχόμενον in the third example is closely connected with the object, αὐτὸν, and expresses an additional action.   The grammatical functions of the participles in these three examples are essentially different.   Hence, any logical classification of participles must include three classes and must follow closely the above lines of cleavage.

Secondly, the terminology used in describing the three classes is a vital point in a discussion of the participle. We regard the office of the participle in the sentence as the proper basis on which to make a logical classification. So let us take the three examples above and determine what is the chief function of the participle in each sentence.

Πόλις οἰκουμένη may mean an inhabited city, or a city (is) inhabited or a city that is inhabited, or ἡ οἰκουμένη means the (inhabited) world. That is, the participle is used attributively (or relatively), predicatively, and substantively. But in each case the participle ascribes to the substantive a state of action which involves also a characteristic. The city in question is in an inhabited state and possesses the characteristic of being inhabited. Then why not call this class of participles "ascriptive" which is a term comprehensive enough to include all varieties of use found in this class? That is, the first class of participles might well be denominated ascriptive to include all participles which ascribe to a substantive expressed or implied a state growing out of an action, a state involving also a characteristic.

The objection to the term attributive to denominate this class is that it does not cover all the uses of the class (e. g., the predicative and substantive uses) and is also used by most grammarians to refer to a subclass in the main class. Of course, this is illogical, and on the whole the term ascriptive is more fitting than attributive to denominate the first category of participles.

As to the function of the participle in ἐλθὼν εἶδον it evidently takes the place of a dependent clause—when I came, because I came, etc. Because such clauses modify like an adverb the principal verb εἶδον, this participle is called by Burton, Jannaris, etc., the adverbial participle. But it is objectionable to call participles by the names of parts of speech. Yet, on the whole, it is better to call this class adverbial than circumstantial, since all participles express a circumstance in one sense or another. Nor is it fitting to denominate this class predicative, as do Hadley and Allen, because this term does not distinguish it from the third class, nor from part of the first class.

As to the function of the third participle ἐρχόμενον, in ὁράω αὐτὸν ἐρχόμενον, it is clear that αὐτὸν ἐρχόμενον together constitutes the direct object of ὁράω, just as ἄνθρωπον is the direct object of ὁράω ἄνθρωπον. But this is not all the participle does in this sentence. It helps to express an action which is closely connected with αὐτὸν. Hence, it is not true to all the facts to call it a substantive participle, as does Burton, because it helps complete an action in addition to its forming part of the direct object of the verb.

Take two other examples of this third class which are apparently somewhat different as to the function of the participle: ἐπαύσατο λέγων, he ceased speaking. Does the participle express a complement to an object, as in the former example? Before answering this question let us look at a sentence with the active of this verb: ἔπαυσεν αὐτὸν λέγοντα, he stopped him (from) speaking. Here the participle evidently is a part of the object. Then does the participle change its function, because the principal verb has changed its voice? It is not probable that such is the case, for ἐπαύσατο λέγων really means, he stopped himself (from) speaking. Hence, the function of the participle is the same as that in the former example, that is, a part of the object but expressing an additional action.

In the sentence, οἶδε δίκαιος ὤν, he knows that he is right, does the participle constitute a part of the object as in the other examples? Surely it does, for it means, he knows the (fact of) his being right.

Then it seems more fitting to call the third class complementary rather than substantive. It is also better to use the term complementary than the term supplementary, because the latter term expresses an addition that may not be so vitally connected with what goes before, while the term complementary means that which helps to complete what goes before and so is vitally connected with it. This is precisely what the participle in the third class does.

Sec. ii. Terminology Adopted for This Treatise

I. The ascriptive participle, divided further into:

1. The attributive, e. g., ὁ τρέχων ἄνθρωπος, the running man, or the man who runs.

2. The predicative, e. g., ὁ διδάσκαλός ἐστι διδάσκων, the teacher is teaching.

3. The substantive, where the substantive is implied and the participle has a substantive meaning, e. g., ἡ οἰκουμένη, the (inhabited) world; ὁ πιστεύων, the believer.

II. The adverbial participle, which is usually equivalent to a subordinate clause, but sometimes equivalent to a phrase of manner or means. Often the adverbial participial clause is only general in its nature and does not make prominent the relation of the subordinate clause to the principal sentence. Again the adverbial participle, by the aid of the context, particularizes the relation of the subordinate clause to the principal sentence and then we have adverbial participles of time, cause, condition, concession, etc.   Hence, we designate the subclasses of adverbials as general, temporal, causal, those of manner or means, concession, condition, and purpose.

III. The complementary participle, which is used with verbs of perceiving, emotion, beginning, continuing, ceasing, etc.   There are two subclasses:

1. The objective complementary participle in which the participle belongs to an object other than the subject of the clause: e. g., ἤκουσα αὐτοῦ λαλοῦντος, I heard him speaking; ἤκουσα τὸ στράτευμα ἐρχόμενον, I heard that the army was coming.

2. The subjective complementary participle in which the action belongs to an object unexpressed because identical with the subject of the clause: e. g., ἐπαύσατο λέγων, he ceased speaking; οἶδε δίκαιος ὤν, he knows that he is right.

It is to be observed that in John 4:39 the complementary participle is used as a limiting genitive.   The same construction is found in Heb. 8:9, but is rare in general Greek literature and does not occur in the Book of Acts.

The above subclasses may be divided further into complementary participles not in indirect discourse and those in indirect discourse.

CHAPTER II

A COMPARATIVE STUDY OF GREEK PARTICIPLES

SEC. 12

The student of New Testament participles naturally asks, What is the use of the participle in other Greek literature? Is there an evolution of participial usage?

Three divisions of Greek literature outside the New Testament, covering the period from Homer to Plutarch, are studied: the Early Greek literature from Homer to Plato, the Late, or κοινή, Greek literature from Polybius to Plutarch, and the documentary papyri.

A thousand lines in each author have been examined, since we deem this a sufficient amount to let any author exhibit his participial usage. In the papyri we take documentary fragments amounting in all to one thousand lines. We have adopted as our standard page in this treatise the page of thirty lines, since this is about the average page in WH edition of the New Testament.

SEC. 13. THE USE OF THE PARTICIPLE IN HOMER (*ca.* 950–850 B. C.) (*Iliad*, BOOK I, ed. Seymour, 1903)

In a thousand lines of Homer's *Iliad* occur only 272 participles, an average of $8\frac{1}{8}$ per page. Thirty-nine of these ($14\frac{1}{3}$ per cent.) are ascriptive; 214 ($78\frac{2}{3}$ per cent.) adverbial; 10 (*ca.* 7 per cent.) complementary.

SEC. 14. THE USE OF THE PARTICIPLE IN SOPHOCLES (d. *ca.* 433 B. C.) (*Antigone*, ed. D'Ooge, 1890; *Oed. Tyr.*, ed. Earle, 1901)

One thousand lines from *Antigone* and *Oedipus Tyrannus* together contain 301 participles, an average of a little over 9 per page. Seventy-eight of these ($25\frac{5}{6}$ per cent.) are ascriptive; 175 ($58\frac{1}{7}$ per cent.) adverbial; 48 (about 16 per cent.) complementary. There are fewer participles in *Oedipus Tyrannus* than in *Antigone* in the ratio of 145 to 156. There are also fewer complementary participles in *Oedipus Tyrannus* than in *Antigone* in the ratio of 22 to 26.

SEC. 15. THE USE OF THE PARTICIPLE IN HERODOTUS (d. *ca.* 425 B. C.) (Book I, ed. Sayce, 1883)

One thousand lines contain 585 participles, an average of $17\frac{1}{2}$ per page. One hundred forty-one of these ($24\frac{1}{10}$ per cent.) are ascriptive; 414 ($70\frac{4}{5}$ per cent.) adverbial; 30 ($5\frac{1}{10}$ per cent.) complementary.

SEC. 16. THE USE OF THE PARTICIPLE IN THUCYDIDES (d. *ca.* 400 B. C.)
(From *Sicilian Expedition*, ed. Frost, 1896)

In one thousand lines occur 432 participles, an average of nearly 13 per page. Ninety-six of these ($22\frac{2}{5}$ per cent.) are ascriptive; 313 ($72\frac{1}{5}$ per cent.) adverbial; 23 ($5\frac{2}{5}$ per cent.) complementary.

SEC. 17. THE USE OF THE PARTICIPLE IN XENOPHON (d. after 355 B. C.)
(*Anab.*, Book I, ed. Kelsey and *Zenos* after text of Cobet)

One thousand lines contain 413 participles, an average of $12\frac{2}{5}$ per page. One hundred seventeen of these (*ca.* $28\frac{1}{3}$ per cent.) are ascriptive; 272 (*ca.* $65\frac{5}{7}$ per cent.) adverbial; 24 (nearly 6 per cent.) complementary.

SEC. 18. THE USE OF THE PARTICIPLE IN PLATO (d. 347 B. C.)
(*Gorgias*, ed. Lodge, 1896; *Republic*, ed. Hermann-Teubner, 1896; *Laws*, ed. Hermann-Teubner, 1899)

One thousand lines (one-third from each of the above works) contain 339 participles, an average of $10\frac{1}{3}$ per page. One hundred fifty-two of these ($45\frac{1}{2}$ per cent.) are ascriptive; 183 ($50\frac{1}{7}$ per cent.) adverbial; 17 ($4\frac{6}{7}$ per cent.) complementary.

SEC. 19. THE USE OF THE PARTICIPLE IN DEMOSTHENES (d. 322 B. C.)
(*Olynthiacs* A and B, ed. Sandys, 1898)

In one thousand lines occur 358 participles, an average of $10\frac{3}{4}$ per page. One hundred forty of these ($37\frac{1}{8}$ per cent.) are ascriptive; 185 (nearly $51\frac{3}{4}$ per cent.) adverbial; 33 (*ca.* $11\frac{1}{4}$ per cent.) complementary.

SEC. 20. THE USE OF THE PARTICIPLE IN THE SEPTUAGINT (*ca.* 280 f. ?)

In one thousand lines from Exod., chaps. 1–7, Deut., chaps. 28–31 (discourse, to even up the narrative, since we find both discourse and narrative in the Book of Acts), and from Judg., chaps. 1–5, we find only 205 participles, an average of *ca.* $6\frac{1}{8}$ per page. Most of them, that is, 160 (78 per cent.), are ascriptive. Only 41 (20 per cent.) are adverbial, while only about 2 per cent. are complementary.

Of course, this is simply translation Greek and the style is largely influenced by the Hebrew. A little less than one-half of the participles in the Septuagint translate participles in the Hebrew, that is, over half of the participles in the Septuagint translate something else (infinitive absolute, infinitive construct, or a finite verb). Yet, a little over one-half of the participles in the Hebrew are not translated by participles in the Septuagint, some being translated by substantives and some by finite verbs. It is especially to be observed that eighteen of the adverbials in the Septuagint translate the Hebrew infinitive construct לֵאמֹר. Yet, many times in the Septuagint λέγων, or λέγοντες, occurs where the infinitive construct of the verb of saying is not found in the Hebrew.

All the participles in Hebrew are ascriptive or used for the finite verb to express continuous action (so Harper). The Hebrews knew not the adverbial use of the participle until they learned it from Greek-speaking peoples. The forty-one cases of the adverbial, and the four cases of the complementary, participles in the Septuagint show how the translators were influenced by Hellenism (as to grammatical constructions at least).

SEC. 21. THE USE OF THE PARTICIPLE IN POLYBIUS (d. *ca.* 125 B. C.)
(*Hist.*, ed. Büttner-Wobst after L. Dindorfio)

One thousand lines contain 593 participles, an average of $17\frac{4}{5}$ per page. One hundred sixty-four of these ($27\frac{3}{4}$ per cent.) are ascriptive; 414 ($69\frac{4}{5}$ per cent.) adverbial; 15 (*ca.* $2\frac{1}{2}$ per cent.) complementary.

SEC. 22. THE USE OF THE PARTICIPLE IN II MACCABEES (date bet.·
Polybius and Strabo; ed. Swete, O. T. in Greek)

One thousand lines contain 781 participles, an average of nearly $23\frac{1}{2}$ per page. Two hundred seventy-four of these (a little over 35 per cent.) are ascriptive; 487 (a little over $62\frac{1}{3}$ per cent.) adverbial; 20 (a little less than $2\frac{2}{3}$ per cent.) complementary.

SEC. 23. THE USE OF THE PARTICIPLE IN STRABO (d. *ca.* 24 A. D.)
(*Geog.*, Books V ff.; Description of Italy, etc.; ed. Meineke, 1868)

In one thousand lines we find 453 participles, an average of a little over $13\frac{1}{2}$ per page. Two hundred twelve of these ($46\frac{4}{5}$ per cent.) are ascriptive; 233 (nearly $51\frac{1}{2}$ per cent.) adverbial; only 8 ($1\frac{7}{10}$ per cent.) complementary.

SEC. 24. THE USE OF THE PARTICIPLE IN JOSEPHUS (d. *ca.* 100 A. D.)
(*Antiq.*, Books XII and XIII, ed. Niese, 1888–92)

In one thousand lines occur 667 participles, an average of 20 per page. One hundred eleven of these ($16\frac{2}{3}$ per cent.) are ascriptive; 520 (nearly 78 per cent.) adverbial; 36 ($5\frac{1}{3}$ per cent.) complementary.

SEC. 25. THE USE OF THE PARTICIPLE IN PLUTARCH (d. *ca.* 125 A. D.)
(*The Life of Pericles*, ed. Holden, 1894)

One thousand lines contain 466 participles, an average of nearly 14 per page. One hundred thirty-five of these (nearly 29 per cent.) are ascriptive; 304 (nearly $65\frac{1}{4}$ per cent.) adverbial; 27 (*ca.* $5\frac{3}{4}$ per cent.) complementary.

SEC. 26. THE USE OF THE PARTICIPLE IN THE DOCUMENTARY PAPYRI (From *Catalog of Greek Papyri*, Vol. II, Rom. Period, 1st cent. A. D., and part from *Oxyrhyncus Papyri*, Grenfell and Hunt, 1st cent. A. D.)

In one thousand lines of these fragments occur only 228 participles, an average of only $6\frac{84}{100}$. One hundred ninety-two of these ($84\frac{1}{4}$ per cent.) are ascriptive; 32 (*ca.* 14 per cent.) adverbial; 4 (*ca.* $2\frac{3}{4}$ per cent.) complementary.

On the next page is given a table recapitulating the facts concerning the participle in all the authors examined in this chapter. Then some observations and comparisons based on these figures will be made, thus paving the way for still further facts and consequent comparisons.

SEC. 27. GENERAL RECAPITULATIVE TABLE OF GREEK PARTICIPLES

Author	Date	Lines	Total Participles	Average per Page of 30 lines	Ascriptive Per cent.	Adverbial Per cent.	Complementary Per cent.
Homer.......	c. 950–850 B. C.	1,000	272	$8\frac{1}{8}$	$14\frac{1}{8}$	$78\frac{2}{3}$	7
Herodotus ...	d. 425 B. C.	1,000	585	$17\frac{1}{2}$	$24\frac{1}{10}$	$70\frac{2}{3}$	$5\frac{1}{10}$
Sophocles....	d. 433 B. C.	1,000	301	9+	$25\frac{5}{8}$	$58\frac{1}{7}$	16
Thucydides..	d. 400 B. C.	1,000	432	13	$22\frac{5}{8}$	$72\frac{1}{3}$	$5\frac{5}{8}$
Xenophon ...	d. *ca.* 355 B. C.	1,000	413	$12\frac{3}{8}$	$28\frac{1}{3}$	$65\frac{5}{6}$	6–
Plato........	d. 347 B. C.	1,000	339	$10\frac{1}{3}$	$45\frac{1}{2}$	$50\frac{1}{4}$	$4\frac{4}{5}$
Demosthenes.	d. 322 B. C.	1,000	358	$10\frac{3}{4}$	$37\frac{3}{8}$	$51\frac{2}{3}$	c. $11\frac{1}{4}$
Septuagint...	......	....	....	...	...	..	..
(Ex., Dt., Jg.)	280 f. B. C.	1,000	205	$6\frac{1}{8}$	78	20	2
Polybius.....	d. 125 B. C.	1,000	593	$17\frac{4}{5}$	$27\frac{2}{3}$	$69\frac{4}{5}$	$2\frac{1}{2}$
II Maccabees.	150–100 B. C.	1,000	781	$23\frac{1}{2}$	35	$62\frac{2}{5}$	$2\frac{2}{3}$
Strabo.......	d. *ca.* 24 A. D.	1,000	453	$13\frac{1}{2}$	$46\frac{3}{4}$	$51\frac{1}{2}$	$1\frac{7}{10}$
Josephus.....	d. *ca.* 100 A. D.	1,000	667	20	$16\frac{2}{3}$	78	$5\frac{1}{3}$
Plutarch.....	d. *ca.* 125 A. D.	1,000	466	14	29	$65\frac{1}{4}$	$5\frac{3}{4}$
Papyri.......	1st cent. A. D.	1,000	228	$6\frac{4}{5}+$	$84\frac{1}{4}$	14	$2\frac{1}{4}$

SEC. 28. SOME OBSERVATIONS ON THE ABOVE TABLE

1. From this table we observe that the adverbial participle was well developed in Homer, over three-fourths of his participles being adverbial. The complementary participle is also fairly well developed in Homer. Since the Hebrews did not use either the adverbial or complementary participle, these facts show the Greek language in Homer's day to be in an advanced stage in the evolution of its participle, while the Hebrews were in a very low state of participial usage. This conclusion is based on the premise that the ascriptive use of the participle is its original use, which is doubtless true.

2. In Sophocles the tragic poet the average is very small—a little over 9 per page. But he has the largest proportion of complementary parti-

ciples found in any author examined, from Homer to Plutarch. The participle in this author shows a high degree of development both as to its adverbial and its complementary participle. The small average is partially due to the lack of narrative.

3. In the historians, we notice a much larger average in Herodotus—17½—but not so large an average in Thucydides and Xenophon. Hence the nature of the literary form does not entirely account for the difference in average, which is partially due to the individual characteristic of the author. Herodotus uses more ascriptives than Homer, but the adverbial participle is well illustrated in Herodotus and the complementary is fairly common. In Thucydides we find a very large proportion of adverbials—the third largest from Homer to Plutarch (Homer and Josephus excelling him), while the complementary is fairly common. Xenophon is close to Thucydides in his proportion of the three classes, using just a few more ascriptives and just a few less adverbials.

4. Plato goes still farther in using ascriptives. His small number of adverbials is partially due to the non-narrative form of his writings. Demosthenes has a large number of complementary participles—the second largest from Homer to Plutarch; he has also the second largest proportion of ascriptives in any classical author. The adverbial participle is fairly well represented in Plato and Demosthenes, and doubtless its comparatively small number is partially accounted for by the absence of pure narrative in long passages.

5. In Polybius two things are noticeable, his large average and his very small number of complementary participles. II Maccabees is remarkable for its very large average—the largest in any author from Homer to Plutarch—and its very small number of complementaries. Strabo uses nearly as many ascriptives as adverbials, but scarcely any complementaries. Josephus shows two remarkable characteristics, a copious use of the participle and an apparently special effort to use adverbials in imitation of classical and κοινή writers. He surpasses, in number of adverbials, Thucydides and Polybius, and equals Homer, while he uses a fair proportion of complementary participles. Plutarch has about an average κοινή usage, except his average per page is nearer to that of the classical writers.

6. Comparing the participial usage of the classical period with that of the κοινή writers, we notice a much more copious use of the participle in the literary κοινή. The five κοινή writers examined average 18 per page, the six authors of the classical period, only ca. 12 per page. Each group averages ca. 30 per cent. ascriptive, while the former group averages only

61 per cent. adverbial, the latter, 65 per cent.; the former, 9 per cent. com-plementary, the latter, 5 per cent.

7. In the papyri, the language of the masses in everyday life, we find a minimum use of the participle, especially of adverbial and complementary participles which belong to the embellishments of literary style.

The Septuagint has the smallest average of any Greek tested. This is due to the influence of the Hebrew and the vernacular proclivities of the translators. For other observations on the Septuagint see Sec. 20.

CHAPTER III
ENUMERATION OF THE PARTICIPLES IN THE BOOK OF ACTS
SEC. 29. IN CHAPTERS 1-12

The frequency of the participle in Acts is striking even to the superficial reader. To the careful student there is much significance in the use of the participle in Acts. Let us gather the facts.

In the first twelve chapters occur 477 participles to 959 lines (WH), an average of $15\frac{1}{8}$ per page.[1] One hundred sixty-five of these ($34\frac{7}{12}$ per cent.) are ascriptive; 275 ($57\frac{5}{8}$ per cent.) adverbial; 37 (*ca.* $7\frac{3}{4}$ per cent.) complementary. This enumeration follows closely the reading of WH, except we count ἀναστάς in 9:11 with good MS evidence, though WH place it in the margin with ἀνάστα in the text.

The complementary participles in chaps. 1-12 are construed with the following verbs: ἀκούω, βλέπω, ἐπιμένω, εὑρίσκω, θεάομαι, θεωρέω, ὁράω (εἶδον), παύομαι, καλῶς ποιέω.

SEC. 30. PARTICIPLES IN THE PETRINE ADDRESSES

In Peter's address at the election of Matthias, 1:16-22, occur 7 participles to $14\frac{1}{2}$ lines, including vss. 18 and 19 which are doubtful and which contain 2 participles. Calvin, B. and J. Weiss, and Feine regard vss. 18 and 19 as an "improper interpolation into the speech." Blass thinks it wanting in the B-text, because it is not cited by Irenaeus when quoting vss. 16-20. Wendt and other exegetes hesitate. The results are nearly the same, whether we regard these verses in or out of the address. That is, if we count $14\frac{1}{2}$ lines (omitting the quotation) the average is $14\frac{1}{2}$ per page, 5 ($71\frac{3}{7}$ per cent.) ascriptive; 2 ($28\frac{4}{7}$ per cent.) adverbial. If we count 10 lines (omitting 18 and 19) the average is 15, 4 (80 per cent.) ascriptive; one (20 per cent.) adverbial. We notice, comparing the figures with those above, that the longer form of the address agrees more nearly with the whole first portion (chaps. 1-12).

The address at Pentecost, 2:14b-36, contains 12 participles to 28 lines (omitting 16 lines from Joel and 8 lines from the Psalms in which 24 lines there is not a single participle), an average of $12\frac{6}{7}$. Five of these ($41\frac{2}{3}$ per cent.) are ascriptive; 7 ($58\frac{1}{3}$ per cent). adverbial. These figures are near to those of chaps. 1-12, except there are no complementary participles, their percentage going to the ascriptive.

In the address from Solomon's porch, 3:12b-26, occur 7 participles to 26 lines (omitting 8 lines which are quoted from Genesis and Deuteronomy),

[1] Page means 30 lines throughout this treatise.

13

an average of $8\frac{1}{13}$ per page. Two of these ($28\frac{4}{7}$ per cent.) are ascriptive; 5 ($71\frac{3}{7}$ per cent.) adverbial.

In the address to the Sanhedrin, 4:8b–12, occur 4 participles (all ascriptive) to 10 lines, an average of 12 per page.

We omit addresses containing less than 6 lines as too short for consideration. In the address before the Sanhedrin after the release from prison, 5:29b–32, occur 2 participles to 6 lines, an average of 10 per page, half ascriptive, half adverbial.

In his address to Simon Magus, 8:20b–23, occurs only one participle (complementary) to $6\frac{1}{2}$ lines, an average of only 5 per page. The address to Cornelius' household, 10:34b–43, contains 13 participles to 22 lines, an average of $17\frac{8}{11}$ per page, 8 ($61\frac{7}{13}$ per cent.) ascriptive; 5 ($38\frac{6}{13}$ per cent.) adverbial. This is the largest average in the Petrine addresses.

In the address to the apostles and Jerusalem Christians, 11:5–17, occur 12 participles to $25\frac{1}{2}$ lines, an average of $14\frac{1}{8}$ per page, the ascriptive, adverbial, and complementary each claiming one-third. Only one other Petrine address (that to Simon Magus) contains a complementary participle (and that only one, but all contained in the address).

In the address to the Jerusalem Conference, 15:7–11, which belongs logically to the Petrine portion, occur only 2 participles to 10 lines, an average of only 6 per page, both adverbial. These striking facts, and those concerning all the addresses will be discussed later.

SEC. 31. THE PARTICIPLE IN GAMALIEL'S ADDRESS (5:35b–39)

This address contains 12 lines, but has only one participle, adverbial, an average of only $2\frac{1}{2}$ per page.

SEC. 32. THE PARTICIPLES IN STEPHEN'S ADDRESS (7:2–53)

This address contains 34 participles to 100 lines (excluding 19 lines of matter quoted directly in which occurs one participle, ἰδών, vs. 34, not counted here), an average of 11 per page. Eleven of these ($34\frac{4}{5}$ per cent.) are ascriptive; 21 ($59\frac{4}{5}$ per cent.) adverbial; 2 ($5\frac{3}{5}$ per cent.) complementary. Of course, much of the 100 lines is colored with Septuagint phraseology.

SEC. 33. PARTICIPLES IN THE SECOND PORTION, CHAPS. 13–28

These chapters contain 806 participles to 1,272 lines, an average of 19 per page. One hundred ninety-four of these (ca. 24 per cent.) are ascriptive; 590 (nearly $73\frac{1}{2}$ per cent.) adverbial; 22 (ca. $2\frac{1}{2}$ per cent.) complementary. The complementary participles in this portion are construed with the following verbs: ἀκούω, γινώσκω, διατελέω, εἶδον, ἐπίσταμαι, εὑρίσκω, θεωρέω, παύομαι.

In the first portion nine different verbs took the complementary participle, but eight take it in the second portion. The verbs that take it in the second portion take it also in the first, except γινώσκω, διατελέω and ἐπίσταμαι. The verbs that take it in the first portion take it also in the second, except βλέπω, ἐπιμένω, θεάομαι, and καλῶς ποιέω.

On comparing the two portions of the Book of Acts as to number and nature of participles, we see that chaps. 1–12 average 15⅛ per page, while the average of chaps. 13–28 is 19—over 26 per cent. larger. Chaps. 1–12 contain 34$\frac{7}{12}$ per cent. ascriptive participles, while chaps. 13–28, only *ca.* 24 per cent. The first portion contains only 57⅞ per cent. adverbial participles, while the second portion has *ca.* 73½ per cent. The first twelve chapters contain 7¾ per cent. complementary participles, while the remaining chapters have only 2½ per cent. These facts are striking when we first face them. But we will wait till we come to Part II to draw conclusions from them.

SEC. 34. PARTICIPLES IN THE PAULINE ADDRESSES

Six lines are still regarded as the minimum for an address. The first address of Paul, that in the synagogue of Pisidian Antioch, 13:16*b*–41, contains 20 participles to 40 lines (10 lines of quoted matter with one participle not counted), an average of 15 per page. Twelve of these (60 per cent.) are ascriptive; 8 (40 per cent.) adverbial.

His address to the Lystrans, 14:15–17 (ascribed to Paul and Barnabas, but Paul was doubtless the chief speaker), contains only 7 lines (excluding the quotation) with 6 participles, half ascriptive and half adverbial. This is an average of 25$\frac{5}{7}$ per page, the largest average we have found so far.

The address to the Athenians, 17:22*b*–31, has 15 participles to 23 lines, an average of 19½ per page. Three of these (20 per cent.) are ascriptive; 12 (80 per cent.) adverbial.

The address to the Ephesian elders, 20:18*b*–35, has 19 participles to 37 lines, an average of 15½ per page. Ten of these (52⅔ per cent.) are ascriptive; 9 (47⅓ per cent.) adverbial.

The address to the Jewish people in Aramaic, 22:1, 3–21, has 35 participles to 42 lines, an average of 25 per page. Eighteen of these (51$\frac{3}{7}$ per cent.) are ascriptive; 15 (42$\frac{6}{7}$ per cent.) adverbial; 2 (5$\frac{5}{7}$ per cent.) complementary. We must stop to say, this is a high average for a speech purporting to be delivered originally in Aramaic, unless it be a free composition by some later hand. Paul's reported words in 23:1, 3, 5, 6, are not to be counted as an address, since they occur in a dialogue.

The address before Felix in reply to Tertullus, 24:10*b*–21, has 13 participles to 22 lines, an average of 17$\frac{8}{11}$ per page. One of these (7$\frac{9}{13}$

per cent.) is ascriptive (the smallest percentage of ascriptives anywhere yet found); 8 ($61\frac{7}{13}$ per cent.) adverbial; 4 ($30\frac{10}{13}$ per cent.) complementary.

Paul's words to Festus, 25:8, 10, 11, containing only five lines, do not constitute an address proper. His address to Agrippa, 26:2–23, has 24 participles to 49 lines, an average of $14\frac{5}{7}$ per page. Seven of these ($29\frac{1}{6}$ per cent.) are ascriptive; 15 ($62\frac{1}{2}$ per cent.) adverbial; 2 ($8\frac{1}{3}$ per cent.) complementary.

His address to the ship's crew and passengers, 27:21–26, contains 3 participles to 10 lines, an average of 9 per page, one-third ascriptive and two-thirds adverbial. His other words during the storm are not counted (27:10, 33, 34).

His last recorded address in Acts, 28:17–20, contains 4 participles to $8\frac{3}{4}$ lines, averaging $13\frac{1}{11}$ per page, all being adverbial. Although Paul is represented as speaking, 28:25–28, these words are not counted because most of this section is a quotation, and only two or three lines are assumed to be Paul's original words.

Sec. 35. Participles in the Addresses at the Jerusalem Conference

For Peter's address see p. 13 above (only two participles in 10 lines and both adverbial).

James's address, 15:13b–21, has only eight lines (excluding the long direct quotation from Amos) with 3 participles, 2 ascriptive and one adverbial. This is an average of $11\frac{1}{4}$ per page. The letter of James averages 10 per page, $71\frac{3}{7}$ per cent. ascriptive and $28\frac{4}{7}$ per cent. adverbial.

Sec. 36. The Participles in the Letter of Decrees

The letter containing the so-called decrees of the "apostles and elders to the brothers of the Gentiles in Antioch and Syria and Cilicia," 15:23b–29, contains 6 participles to 13 lines, an average of $13\frac{11}{13}$ per page, one ($16\frac{2}{3}$ per cent.) ascriptive; 5 ($83\frac{1}{3}$ per cent.) adverbial. Γενομένοις, 15:25, may be ascriptive instead of adverbial, changing the percentage to $33\frac{1}{3}$ ascriptive, $66\frac{2}{3}$ adverbial.

Sec. 37. The Participles in the Non-Christian Addresses

The first of these, that of Demetrius to the workmen in Ephesus, 19:25b–27, has four participles to eight and one-half lines, an average of ca. $14\frac{1}{8}$ per page, 2 ascriptive, the others adverbial.

The address of the Ephesian town clerk, 19:35b–40, contains 6 participles to 12 lines, an average of 15 to the page, one-third ascriptive, one-half adverbial, and one-sixth complementary.

Lysias' letter to Felix, 23:26–30, has 9 participles to 10 lines, an average of 27 per page (the largest average found in our investigations in or out of the New Testament). Seven ($77\frac{7}{9}$ per cent.) of these are adverbial; 2 ($22\frac{2}{9}$ per cent.) are complementary, while there is not an ascriptive participle in the letter. This is the only piece of Greek examined (except Gamaliel's short-speech with only one adverbial participle) that does not contain an ascriptive participle.

Tertullus' address against Paul, 24:2b–8, contains 6 participles to 10 lines, one-third ascriptive and two-thirds adverbial. Its average per page is 18.

Festus' address to Agrippa, in two parts, 25:14b–21 and 25:24–27, has 16 participles to 27 lines, an average of $17\frac{7}{9}$ per page. Four of these (25 per cent.) are ascriptive; 12 (75 per cent.) adverbial.

SEC. 38. THE PARTICIPLES IN THE "WE" PASSAGES

In 16:10–17 (the journey from Troas to Philippi and some events in the latter) occur 15 participles to 21 lines, an average of 20 per page. Six of these (40 per cent.) are ascriptive; 9 (60 per cent.) adverbial. The 21 lines immediately preceding 16:10 have 12 participles, $41\frac{2}{3}$ per cent. ascriptive and $58\frac{1}{3}$ per cent. adverbial. The 21 lines immediately following 16:17 have 13 participles, only one of which is ascriptive, the rest being adverbial. That is, there is a similarity of participial usage between this "We" passage and its context, not so striking in the nature of the participle but more striking in the number used.

In 20:5–16 (the journey from Philippi to Miletus some years later) occur 23 participles to 27 lines, averaging $25\frac{1}{2}$ per page. Seven of these ($30\frac{2}{3}$ per cent.) are ascriptive; the rest being adverbial. The 27 lines immediately preceding 20:5 have 18 participles, an average of 20 to the page, 2 ascriptive, 15 adverbial, and one complementary. The 27 lines immediately following 20:16 have only 10 participles, an average of 11 to the page, 40 per cent. ascriptive and 60 per cent. adverbial. But we must remember that these last 27 lines belong to Paul's address to the Ephesian elders.

In 21:1–18 (the journey from Miletus to Jerusalem) occur 31 participles to 40 lines, an average of $23\frac{1}{4}$ per page. Five of these ($16\frac{1}{8}$ per cent.) are ascriptive; 26 ($83\frac{7}{8}$ per cent.) adverbial. The 40 lines just before 21:1 have 22 participles, an average of $16\frac{1}{2}$ per page. Nine of these ($40\frac{10}{11}$ per cent.) are ascriptive; 12 ($54\frac{6}{11}$ per cent.) adverbial; one ($4\frac{6}{11}$ per cent.) complementary. Observe, 35 of these last 40 lines belong to Paul's address to the Ephesian elders. The 40 lines immediately following 21:18 have 24 participles, an average of 18 per page. Seven of these ($29\frac{1}{6}$ per cent.) are ascriptive; 16 ($66\frac{2}{3}$ per cent.) adverbial; one ($4\frac{1}{6}$ per cent.) complementary.

In 27:1—28:16 (the sea voyage from Caesarea to Rome) occur 102 participles to 127 lines, an average of $24\frac{1}{10}$ per page. Seventeen of these ($16\frac{2}{3}$ per cent.) are ascriptive; 82 ($80\frac{2}{3}$ per cent.) adverbial; 3 ($2\frac{4}{18}$ per cent.) complementary. The 127 lines immediately before 27:1 have only 65 participles (less than two-thirds as many as the "We" passage), 15 ($23\frac{1}{13}$ per cent.) ascriptive; 48 ($73\frac{11}{13}$ per cent.) adverbial; 2 ($3\frac{1}{13}$ per cent.) complementary. Observe, there is a falling-off of adverbial participles in this context. But, notice, it includes Paul's addresses before Festus and Agrippa, and Festus' address to Agrippa.

Sec. 39.   The Three Accounts of Saul's Conversion

In the first account (first in the book), 9:1–19a, occur 21 participles to 37 lines, an average of *ca.* 17 per page. Seven of these ($33\frac{1}{3}$ per cent.) are ascriptive; 11 ($52\frac{3}{8}$ per cent.) adverbial; 3 ($14\frac{2}{8}$ per cent.) complementary.

In the second account, 22:4–16, occur 20 participles to 27 lines, an average of $22\frac{1}{4}$. Seven of these (35 per cent.) are ascriptive; 12 (60 per cent.) adverbial; one (5 per cent.) complementary.

In the third account, 26:9–18, occur 11 participles to 23 lines, an average of $14\frac{1}{2}$ per page. Two of these ($18\frac{2}{11}$ per cent.) are ascriptive; 7 ($63\frac{7}{11}$ per cent.) adverbial; 2 ($18\frac{2}{11}$ per cent.) complementary.

Sec. 40.   Quoted Matter in the First Portion

We shall count as quoted matter nothing but whole lines (or lines lacking only one or two words) which constitute direct quotations.

In the first twelve chapters of the Book of Acts occur 51 lines of quoted matter, in which are found six participles, an average of only $3\frac{1}{2}$ per page, all being ascriptive.

Sec. 41.   Quoted Matter in the Second Portion

In chaps. 13–28 occur 27 lines of quoted matter, in which are found only 4 participles, an average of $4\frac{4}{9}$ per page, 3 ascriptive, the fourth being a participle which translates the Hebrew infinitive absolute, which is of the nature of the adverbial participle.

One line is from a heathen poet, the rest from the Old Testament (Septuagint likely).

Three of the participles in the citations of chaps. 1–12 translate participles in both Septuagint and Hebrew. The other three do not translate participles either in the Septuagint or the Hebrew.

Of the four participles in the citations of chaps. 13–28 two translate participles in the Hebrew, one translates a substantive, and the fourth, an infinitive absolute. All four, as found in Acts, chaps. 13–28, reproduce participles in the Septuagint. It is most probable that all these quotations were made from the Septuagint.

Sec. 42. Table of Participles in the Book of Acts

Name of Address	Lines	Number of Parti-ciples	Average per Page of 30 Lines	Ascriptive Per cent.	Adverbial Per cent.	Comple-mentary Per cent.
Peter's, at Election of Matthias, 1:16–22	$14\frac{1}{2}$ (10)	7 (5)	$14\frac{1}{2}$ (15)	$71\frac{3}{7}$ (80)	$28\frac{4}{7}$ (20)	..
Peter's, at Pentecost, 2:14*b*–36	28	12	$12\frac{6}{7}$	$41\frac{2}{3}$	$58\frac{1}{3}$	..
Peter's, from Solomon's Porch, 3:12*b*–26	26	7	$8\frac{1}{13}$	$28\frac{4}{7}$	$71\frac{3}{7}$	..
Peter's, to Sanhedrin before Imprisonment, 4:8*b*–12	10	4	12	100	....	..
Peter's, to Sanhedrin after Release, 5:29*b*–32	6	2	10	50	50	..
Peter's, to Simon Magus, 8:20*b*–23	$6\frac{1}{2}$	1	5–	....	....	100
Peter's, to Cornelius' Household, 10:34*b*–43	22	13	$17\frac{8}{11}$	$61\frac{7}{13}$	$38\frac{6}{13}$	..
Peter's, to Apostles and Jerusalem Christians, 11:5–17	$25\frac{1}{2}$	12	$14\frac{1}{8}$	$33\frac{1}{3}$	$33\frac{1}{3}$	$33\frac{1}{3}$
Peter's, at Jerusalem Conference 15:7–11	10	2	6	....	100	..
Total and average for Pet. adds	$148\frac{1}{2}$ (144)	59 (57)	$11\frac{4}{5}$+	$48\frac{1}{3}$	$41\frac{2}{3}$	10
Gamaliel's in Sanh. 5:35*b*–39	12	1	$2\frac{1}{2}$	....	100	..
Stephen's, 7:2–53	100	34	11	$34\frac{4}{5}$	$59\frac{4}{5}$	$5\frac{3}{5}$
Total and average for Pet. por	959	477	$15\frac{1}{6}$	$34\frac{7}{12}$	$57\frac{7}{8}$	$7\frac{3}{4}$
Paul's in Pisidian Antioch, 13:16*b*–41	40	20	15	60	40	..
Paul's, to Lystrans, 14:15–17	7	6	$25\frac{5}{7}$	50	50	..
Paul's, to Athenians, 17:22*b*–31	23	15	$19\frac{1}{2}$	20	80	..
Paul's, to Eph. Elders, 20:18*b*–35	37	19	$15\frac{1}{2}$	$52\frac{2}{3}$	$47\frac{1}{3}$	.
Paul's, to Jewish People in Aramaic, 22:1, 3–21	42	35	25	$51\frac{3}{7}$	$42\frac{6}{7}$	$5\frac{5}{7}$
Paul before Felix, 24:10*b*–21	22	13	$17\frac{8}{11}$	$7\frac{9}{13}$	$61\frac{7}{13}$	$30\frac{10}{13}$

TABLE OF PARTICIPLES IN THE BOOK OF ACTS—*Continued*

Name of Address	Lines	Number of Participles	Average per Page of 30 Lines	Ascriptive Per cent.	Adverbial Per cent.	Complementary Per cent.
Paul before Agrippa, 26:2–23..........	49	24	$14\frac{5}{7}$	$29\frac{1}{6}$	$62\frac{1}{2}$	$30\frac{1}{3}$
Paul to Ship's Crew, 27:21–26.........	10	3	9	$33\frac{1}{3}$	$66\frac{2}{3}$	..
Paul, to Jews in Rome, 28:17–20.........	$8\frac{2}{3}$	4	$13\frac{11}{18}$	....	100	..
Total average for Paul's addresses....	$238\frac{2}{3}$	139	$17\frac{1}{3}$	$39\frac{1}{9}$	$54\frac{1}{3}$	$6\frac{13}{24}$
Demetrius to Workmen in Eph., 19:25*b*–27..........	$8\frac{1}{2}$	4	$14\frac{1}{8}$	50	50	..
Town Clerk to Mob, 19:35*b*–40........	12	6	15	$33\frac{1}{3}$	50	$16\frac{2}{3}$
Lysias to Felix, 23:26–30..............	10	9	27	....	$77\frac{7}{9}$	$22\frac{2}{9}$
Tertullus vs. Paul, 24:2*b*–8...........	10	6	18	$33\frac{1}{3}$	$66\frac{2}{3}$	..
Festus to Agrippa, 25:14*b*–21 and 25:24–27............	27	16	$17\frac{7}{9}$	25	75	..
Total and average in non-Christian adds..	$67\frac{1}{2}$	41	$17\frac{4}{5}$	$22\frac{1}{2}$	70	$7\frac{1}{2}$
First "We" pas., 16:10–17............	21	15	20	40	60	..
Second "We" pas., 20:5–16..........	27	23	$25\frac{1}{2}$	$30\frac{2}{5}$	$69\frac{3}{5}$	..
Third "We" pas., 21:1–18..........	40	31	$23\frac{1}{4}$	$16\frac{1}{3}$	$83\frac{2}{3}$	..
Fourth "We" pas., 27:1—28:16.......	127	102	$24\frac{1}{10}$	$16\frac{2}{3}$	$80\frac{2}{5}$	$2\frac{14}{15}$
Average for "We" passages...........	215	171	23+	*ca.*22	*ca.*77	1–
1st. Acct. Saul's Conversion, 9:1–19*a*....	37	21	*ca.*17	$33\frac{1}{3}$	$52\frac{4}{9}$	$14\frac{2}{9}$
Second Acct. Saul's Conversion, 22:4–16	27	20	$22\frac{1}{4}$	35	60	5
Third Acct. Saul's Conversion, 26:9–18	23	11	$14\frac{1}{3}$	$18\frac{2}{11}$	$63\frac{7}{11}$	$18\frac{2}{11}$
James, at Jerus. Conference, 15:13*b*–21..	8	3	$11\frac{1}{4}$	$66\frac{2}{3}$	$33\frac{1}{3}$	..
Total and average for Pauline por.	1272	806	19	*ca.*24	*ca.*$73\frac{1}{2}$	*ca.* $2\frac{1}{2}$

CHAPTER IV

SEC. 43. THE PARTICIPLE IN THE THIRD GOSPEL

Since this book has been regarded the production of the same author that wrote the Book of Acts, we put it first and submit it to a more thorough examination than the other gospels.

In the Third Gospel occur 1,045 participles to 1,884 lines (the genealogy, not having any participles, is not counted in this number). This is an average of *ca.* $16\frac{2}{3}$ per page,[1] 421 ($40\frac{3}{10}$ per cent.) ascriptive; 580 ($55\frac{1}{2}$ per cent.) adverbial; 44 ($4\frac{1}{6}$ per cent.) complementary.[2]

In the first two chapters, which are peculiar to the Third Gospel and which, by their numerous Hebraisms, betray greater dependence on Aramaic sources, occur 91 participles to 248 lines, an average of 11 to the page. Fifty-five of these ($60\frac{4}{9}$ per cent.) are ascriptive; 29 ($31\frac{8}{9}$ per cent.) adverbial; 7 ($7\frac{2}{3}$ per cent.) complementary. It is to be observed that the average is less in these chapters than in the book at large. Furthermore, it is to be noticed that the ascriptive participles are more numerous in this Hebraistic portion.

The preface has 3 participles to 6 lines, an average of 15 per page, 2 ascriptive, one adverbial. But, of course, 6 lines are not sufficient material from which to test the author's participial usage.

SEC. 44. THE PARTICIPLE IN THE OTHER GOSPELS

Five hundred lines from each of the other gospels are examined, since this amount is regarded as sufficient for the testing of the participial usage in these gospels.

In 500 lines of Matthew (1:18—9:11) occur 209 participles, an average of $12\frac{1}{2}$ per page. Ninety-one of these ($43\frac{1}{2}$ per cent.) are ascriptive; 108 ($51\frac{2}{3}$ per cent.) adverbial; 10 ($4\frac{1}{6}$ per cent.) complementary. The Sermon on the Mount, which is included in this section, contains only 51 participles to 220 lines, an average of 7 to the page, 72 per cent. of which are ascriptive. Hence, our impression is that the book at large would show a little

---

[1] Page in this treatise always means 30 lines.

[2] It must be noticed that 15 of these 1,045 in Luke are bracketed by WH, 11 by double brackets, 4 by single brackets. But if all 15 of them should be finally set aside by textual critics, it would not materially affect the general average stated above.

larger average than $12\frac{1}{2}$ and a larger percentage of adverbials than are found in the section tested.

In 500 lines of Mark (1:1—7:3) occur 194 participles, an average of $11\frac{3}{4}$ per page. Sixty-three of these ($32\frac{1}{2}$ per cent.) are ascriptive; 117 ($60\frac{1}{3}$ per cent.) adverbial; 14 ($7\frac{1}{8}$ per cent.) complementary.

In 500 lines of the Fourth Gospel (first part) occur 174 participles, an average of $10\frac{2}{3}$ per page. One hundred twenty-five of these ($71\frac{4}{5}$ per cent.) are ascriptive; 34 (ca. 20 per cent.) adverbial; 15 ($8\frac{1}{6}$ per cent.) complementary.

SEC. 45.   THE PARTICIPLE IN PAUL'S WRITINGS

The letter to the Galatians contains 260 lines with 82 participles, an average of $9\frac{1}{2}$ per page. Fifty-six of these ($68\frac{3}{10}$ per cent.) are ascriptive; 25 ($30\frac{1}{2}$ per cent.) adverbial; one ($1\frac{1}{5}$ per cent.) complementary.

In 500 lines of Romans (5:1—15:5) occur 155 participles, an average of $9\frac{3}{10}$ per page. One hundred twenty-two of these ($78\frac{2}{3}$ per cent.) are ascriptive; 32 ($20\frac{2}{3}$ per cent.) adverbial; one (scarcely two-thirds of 1 per cent.) complementary. The section examined includes both argumentative and narrative portions.

In 500 lines of I Cor. (first part) occur 132 participles, an average of ca. 8 per page. Ninety-seven of these ($73\frac{1}{2}$ per cent.) are ascriptive; 34 ($25\frac{3}{4}$ per cent.) adverbial; one (ca. three-fourths of 1 per cent.) complementary.

SEC. 46.   THE PARTICIPLE IN OTHER EPISTLES

The Epistle to the Hebrews contains 660 lines in which occur 307 participles, an average of ca. 14 per page. One hundred seventy-five of these (57 per cent.) are ascriptive; 126 (41 per cent.) adverbial; 6 (ca. 2 per cent.) complementary.

The Epistle of James has 214 lines with 71 participles, an average of nearly 10 per page. Forty-nine of these (69 per cent.) are ascriptive; 22 (31 per cent.) adverbial. There is not a complementary participle in this letter.

The Epistle of First Peter contains 220 lines with 115 participles, an average of $15\frac{3}{4}$ per page. Sixty-three of these (nearly 55 per cent.) are ascriptive; 52 (45 per cent.) adverbial. There is not a complementary participle in this letter. Four or five of its participles may easily be counted either as ascriptive or adverbial.

In First John are contained 239 lines in which occur 52 participles, an average of 6½ per page. Forty-nine of these (94¼ per cent.) are ascriptive; 3 (5¾ per cent.) complementary.[1]

Sec. 47. The Participle in the Apocalypse

In 500 lines, 1:1—10:2, occur 163 participles, an average of 9⅘. One hundred thirty-two of these (81 per cent.) are ascriptive; 16 (9¾ per cent.) adverbial; 15 (9¼ per cent.) complementary. How different the participial usage in Revelation from that in the Gospel or Epistle of John!

Sec. 48. Recapitulative Table for the New Testament

Book	Lines	Participles	Average per Page of 30 Lines	Ascriptive Per cent.	Adverbial Per cent.	Complementary Per cent.
Luke	1,884	1,045	16⅔	40 3/10	55½	4⅕
Mark	500	194	11⅔	32½	60⅓	7⅙
Matthew	500	209	12½	43½	51⅔	4⅚
John	500	174	10⅖	71⅘	20	8⅕
Gal.	260	82	9½	68 3/10	30½	1⅕
I Cor.	500	132	8	73½	25¾	¾
Rom.	500	155	9 3/10	78⅔	20⅔	⅔
Hebrews	660	307	14	57	41	2
James	214	71	10—	69	31	. . .
I Pet.	220	115	15⅔	55	45	. . .
I John	239	52	6½	94¼	. . .	5¾
Apoc.	500	163	9⅘	81	9¾	9¼
Acts	2,231	1,283	17⅙	28¼	68	3¾

Sec. 49. Some Observations on This Table

Excepting the Lukan writings, the Epistle to the Hebrews, and First Peter, the average is small throughout the New Testament. The Book of Acts has the highest average, Luke comes next (only two-thirds of 1 per cent. less), then comes First Peter (only 1 per cent. less than Luke). Paul's average is small, ranging from 8 to 9½ in different letters. The Johannine writings (gospel and epistle) have a still lower average, while the Apocalypse has a greater average than the Pauline writings. Matthew comes fourth in average, then comes Mark. The New Testament average is not very much lower than that of the classical writers, but is very far below the average of *κοινή* writers.

As to the nature of the participle, the Book of Acts has the largest percentage of adverbial participles. Mark comes next, then Luke, Matthew, I Pet., Hebrews, then follow in descending grade James, Paul's letters, the Gospel of John, till the Apocalypse has only 9¾ per cent. and First John

[1] This count for the complementary includes ἐληλυθότα, 4:2, which is a doubtful reading (WH).

none at all. There is a remarkable difference between the Gospel and Epistle of John, the gospel having 20 per cent. adverbial, the epistle none at all. The presence of so much narrative in the gospel and its utter absence in the epistle largely explain this difference.

It is to be noticed that the great majority of New Testament participles are ascriptive (especially if we except the Lukan writings, Mark, and Matthew). The κοινή writings, as a whole, show a much larger percentage of adverbials than of ascriptives. The classical literature exhibits the same fondness for the adverbial participle. But the Septuagint and the papyri exhibit a still greater fondness for the ascriptive participle, both using a very small percentage of adverbials.

CHAPTER V

PARTICLES WITH PARTICIPLES IN THE BOOK OF ACTS

Sec. 50. Preliminary Statement

There are not many particles used with the participles of the Book of Acts. Although the author uses the participle copiously, he uses the particles with participles sparingly.

Ἄν with a participle to represent the indicative or optative with ἄν in conditional sentences, a fairly common construction in classical Greek, does not occur at all in the Book of Acts. The following particles used with the participle in classical Greek are not so used in the Book of Acts: ἄτε, διὰ τοῦτο, εἶτα, ἐνταῦθα, ἐξαίφνης, ἔπειτα, εὐθὺς, μεταξὺ, οἶον, οἶα, ὅμως, ὄντως. Καίπερ, common in classical and κοινή Greek, though it occurs in the New Testament five times (3 in Hebrews, one in Paul, one in II Peter), is conspicuously absent from the Book of Acts.

The particles that may be considered as used with participles are ἄμα, ἤδη, καίτοι, οὔτως, τότε, ὡς, ὥσπερ.

Sec. 51. Ἄμα with Participles in the Book of Acts

This particle occurs only twice in the book and that in the late chapters, 24:26; 27:40. In the former the author is describing the rejection of Paul's message by Felix and the latter's promise to call for him at a convenient season, and adds, ἄμα καὶ ἐλπίζων ὅτι χρήματα δοθήσεται, etc., hoping also that money should be given. The participial clause expresses an additional motive for the extension of Paul's imprisonment, and so the participle is causal. Hence, the particle ἄμα, temporal in its nature, does not necessarily make the participle temporal. Perhaps we can, in this instance, see its temporal force in its connection with ἔμφοβος γενόμενος, that is, along with his fear Felix was also hoping to receive money.

In 27:40 the author is telling how the crew cast off the anchors and left them in the sea, ἄμα ἀνέντες τ. ζευκτηρίας τ. πηδαλίων, at the same time having loosed the bands of the rudders. Here the particle is evidently temporal and strengthens the participle which is also temporal.

Sec. 52. Ἤδη with the Participle in the Book of Acts

This particle occurs only once with the participle, 27:9, ὄντος ἤδη, etc. It is used for emphasis, the danger of the voyage was "already" present. It does not necessarily make the participle temporal, for the participle in this sentence seems to express cause rather than time. The

25

presence of the danger is evidently the occasion of Paul's address which immediately follows.

SEC. 53. Καίτοι WITH THE PARTICIPLE IN THE BOOK OF ACTS

Though this particle is used with the concessive participle in classical Greek, and is clearly so used in Heb. 4:3, it is not so used in the Book of Acts. It occurs only once in the book, 14:17, and here it is more closely connected with the finite verb (ἀφῆκεν) than with the participle (ἀγαθουργῶν).

SEC. 54. Οὗτως WITH THE PARTICIPLE IN THE BOOK OF ACTS

There are only two passages that can possibly be considered as bearing on the participle, 20:11; 20:35. In the former, ὁμιλήσας ἄχρι αὐγῆς οὗτως ἐξῆλθεν, having talked with them till dawn thus he went forth, the particle is in apposition with the idea expressed in the participle, but really modifies the action of the principal verb. That is, the οὗτως points back to the participle, gathers up its force, and brings it forward to describe the circumstances under which Paul went forth from Troas.

In 20:35, ὅτι οὗτως κοπιῶντας δεῖ, etc., that so laboring ye should help the weak, the particle directly modifies the participle, and both together modify the principal verb.

SEC. 55. Τότε WITH THE PARTICIPLE IN THE BOOK OF ACTS

This particle occurs eleven times with the participle in the Book of Acts.[1] But the particle is much more closely connected with the finite verb than with the participle. This seems to be true in every instance.

SEC. 56. Ὡς WITH THE PARTICIPLE IN THE BOOK OF ACTS

This particle is not used in the Book of Acts with the future participle to express purpose, as in classical and κοινή Greek (and in Heb. 13:17). The future participle without ὡς is used three times (8:27; 24:11, 17) to express purpose.

In 1:10, ὡς is to be construed with the finite verb, not with the participle. In 3:12, ὡς . . . . πεποιηκόσιν, the particle is construed with the participle and expresses the *supposed* ground of the wonder. That is, the people were wondering on the supposed ground that Peter and John with their own power had healed the lame beggar.

In 19:34 the WH text puts ὡσεί in single half-brackets, though many editors prefer ὡς. But if ὡς be the correct reading, the construction is an anacoluthon, and the ὡς does not seem to go with the participle κραζόντων (or κράζοντες in Tisch.) but with the phrase ἐπὶ ὥρας δύο, for about two hours.

[1] 4:8; 5:26; 7:4; 13:3, 12; 21:26, 33; 25:12; 26:1; 27:21; 28:1.

In 23:15, ὡς μέλλοντας διαγινώσκειν, Buttmann makes the limitation that of *comparison*.   But it seems to me that the particle here has a meaning closely akin to its usual significance, namely, supposed, or pretended, ground of action.   That is, the conspiring band of Jews say to the council, "Have Paul brought on the *apparent* ground that you are going to investigate his case more thoroughly, but we will slay him while he is being brought."   This is evidently the thought.

In 23:20 and 27:30, ὡς is used to express a supposed basis of action. In 28:19, οὐχ ὡς . . . . ἔχων, not because I had, etc., the particle ὡς seems to strengthen the causal participle ἔχων.   Yet more likely the meaning is, not, as it appears to others, because I have anything to bring against my nation, etc.

SEC. 57.   Ὥσπερ WITH THE PARTICIPLE IN THE BOOK OF ACTS

This particle is used only three times in the book and is apparently not construed with either a finite verb or a participle.   In 2:2 the particle is more closely connected with πνοῆς than with the participle φερομένης which simply modifies πνοῆς as an adjective.   In 3:17 and 11:15, ὥσπερ introduces a clause without any form of the verb expressed.

SEC. 58.   Μή AND Οὐ WITH THE PARTICIPLE IN THE BOOK OF ACTS

The usual negative with participles in the Book of Acts is μή, there being thirteen instances with this particle and only one clear case of οὐ. The usage of the negative with the participle in the Book of Acts, though not in accord with the classical usage, is the regular κοινή usage.   But Gildersleeve has shown that even in earlier Greek μή sometimes encroached on οὐ.   So he calls the larger use of μή in late Greek (second century B. C. on) "an extension and not an innovation."   But this is scarcely true of μή with the participle in the Book of Acts.   Here the usage, if not an actual "innovation," is closely bordering on an "innovation," as compared with the classical usage, since μή is used thirteen times and οὐ but once (7:5, with a concessive participle).

It is true, we find οὐ in a participial clause in 17:27, but it is evident that the negative modifies the adverb μακρὸν and not the participle ὑπάρχοντα. It is noticeable, however, that the participial clause in 17:27 is concessive, just as it is in 7:5.   In 27:20, οὐκ goes with ὀλίγου, not with the participle. In 28:2, οὐ modifies the participle which is purely an adjective.   In 28:19, οὐχ modifies the whole clause introduced by ὡς, and not the participle ἔχων.

CHAPTER VI

THE PERIPHRASTIC PARTICIPLE IN THE BOOK OF ACTS

SEC. 59. PRELIMINARY STATEMENT

The periphrastic construction is often found in the Book of Acts, and is fairly common also in the Third Gospel. Plummer, in his commentary on Luke, p. li, asserts that this construction is a Hebraism. Yet, he admits that "many (cases) would be admissible in classical Greek." It is quite evident from the following facts that the periphrastic construction is no Hebraism. Even as far back as Homer we find this construction, though its occurrences there are rare—only 4 to 1,000 lines. But in Demosthenes we find 14 cases to 1,000 lines, in Polybius, 8 to 1,000 lines, and in Strabo, 15. Perhaps we are safe in inferring from these facts that the periphrastic construction became more common in κοινή writers than in the earlier authors. If so, this would help to account for the excessive use of the periphrastic participle in the Lukan writings. Yet, the fact that Josephus and Plutarch scarcely ever used a periphrastic participle is difficult to explain, unless we regard their Greek abnormal, as it seems to be (especially that of Josephus who uses fewer periphrastic and more adverbial participles than any other κοινή writer).

SEC. 60. VARIOUS FORMS OF THE PERIPHRASTIC PARTICIPLE IN THE BOOK OF ACTS

There are seven different uses—that of the present participle with the present tense of εἶναι (5 occurrences in the book); that of the present participle with the imperfect of εἶναι (33 cases); that of the perfect participle with the present of εἶναι (5 cases); that of the perfect participle with the imperfect of εἶναι (16 cases); that of the present participle with ὑπάρχω (2 cases); that of the perfect participle with ὑπάρχω (2 cases); that of the present participle with the future of the verb to be, ἔσῃ (one case).

Thus we see that there are in all 64 instances of the periphrastic participle in the Book of Acts, an average of a little over 29 to the 1,000 lines. That is, the author of the Book of Acts uses about twice as many periphrastic participles as Demosthenes or Strabo, in whose writings the construction occurs most frequently outside the Book of Acts.

SEC. 61. THE DISTRIBUTION OF PERIPHRASTIC PARTICIPLES IN THE BOOK OF ACTS

Of the 64 occurrences in the book 34 are found in chaps. 1–12 and 30 in chaps. 13–28. That is, though there is about one-third more material in chaps. 13–28, yet there are over 20 per cent. more periphrastic participles in chaps. 1–12. That is, in chaps. 1–12 there is one periphrastic participle to every 26⅔ lines, while in chaps. 13–28 there is one to every 43⅖ lines— about one-third greater average in chaps. 1–12.

Perhaps facts like these are the basis of statements like that of Plummer quoted above. But we are not driven to conclude that, because there are so many periphrastic participles to the page in the Aramaic portion of a book (whether Luke or Acts), therefore the periphrastic construction is a Hebraism. The very fact that it does occur in Homer, Demosthenes, Polybius, and Strabo proves it to be a regular Greek construction and not a Hebraism. On the other hand, the fact that the periphrastic construction is more frequently used in the Aramaic portion of the Book of Acts does lead us to conclude that the periphrastic participle is more common in writings influenced by Aramaic sources than in writings purely Greek in their origin.

SEC. 62. THE FACTS AS TO THE LOCATION AND USE OF PERIPHRASTIC PARTICIPLES IN ACTS, CHAPS. 1–12

If there is only one participle in a verse, it is designated by chapter and verse; if there are more than one in a verse, they are designated by the letters a, b, c, d, e, affixed to the verse number, a standing for the first participle in the verse, b, for the second, etc.

The instances of the present participle with the present of εἰμι are: 1:12b; 4:36b; 5:25c; 10:19b.[1] The instances of the present participle with the imperfect of εἰμι are: 1:10a, 13, 14; 2:3a, 5, 42; 8:1, 13b, 28a, 28b; 9:9, 28a, 28b; 10:24a, 30; 11:5a; 12:5, 6a, 12d, 20a. Perfect participle with the present of εἰμι: 2:13b; 5:25b. Perfect participle with imperfect of εἰμι: 1:17; 4:31b; 8:16a; 9:33b; 12:12c. Present participle with ὑπάρχω: 8:9a, 9b. Perfect participle with ὑπάρχω: 8:16b.

SEC. 63. THE FACTS AS TO THE LOCATION AND USE OF PERIPHRASTIC PARTICIPLES IN ACTS, CHAPS. 13–28

Present participle with the present of εἰμι: 19:36b. Present participle with the imperfect of εἰμι: 14:7; 16:9b, 9c, 12; 18:7c; 19:14; 20:9b;[1] 21:3c, 9; 22:19a, 19b, 20b, 20c. Perfect participle with the present of εἰμι: 21:33b; 25:14b; 26:26b. Perfect participle with the imperfect of εἰμι: 13:48b; 14:26; 16:9a; 18:25a; 19:32; 20:8, 13c; 21:29; 22:20a, 29c; 25:10. Perfect participle with ὑπάρχω (infinitive): 19:36c. Present participle with the future of εἰμι: 13:11a.

[1] Copula omitted.

Sec. 64. Some Observations on These Facts

It is to be observed that nine of the perfect participles with the verb to be are the pluperfect passive. Three of the perfect participles with the present of the verb to be are used as perfect passive. Two of the perfects with the present of the verb to be are active and are used to increase the vividness of the action.

The most common form of the periphrastic participle in the Book of Acts is that of the present participle with the imperfect of the verb to be— a little over half of all the cases are in this form. This form is used in narrative to describe vividly a progressive action in the past. The present participle with the present of the verb to be (five cases in the book) describes vividly a progressive action in the present. The one case of the present participle with the future of the verb to be seems to express vividly a progressive action in the future.

It is to be noticed that not only εἶναι, but also ὑπάρχειν, and προϋπάρχειν take the periphrastic construction in the Book of Acts. In 28:8 occurs συνεχόμενον with κατακεῖσθαι (was lying sick) almost in a periphrastic sense. But it is not counted, because this verb does not regularly take a periphrastic construction.

CHAPTER VII
THE GENITIVE ABSOLUTE IN THE BOOK OF ACTS
SEC. 65. INTRODUCTORY STATEMENT

The genitive absolute seems to have had its origin on Greek soil (so Spieker and Brugmann, *American Journal of Philology*, VI, 310 ff.). It probably arose with the present participle of time, since most of the cases in Homer are such, with only a few aorist absolute genitives. Only a few absolute genitives occur in Homer, a few more in Hesiod, but there is a gradual increase in the use of this construction until it reached its climax in the Attic orators (so Spieker).

SEC. 66. THE FACTS AS TO THE LOCATION AND FUNCTION OF THE GENITIVE ABSOLUTE IN ACTS, CHAPS. 1–12

For the method of locating the participles see first paragraph, Sec. 62.

The following cases of the genitive absolute belong to the general adverbial: 1:9*b;* 3:11*a;* 5:2*a;* 10:10; total, 4. Cases implying time: 1:10*b;* 6:1; 7:30, 31*b;* 10:9*a,* 9*b,* 19*a,* 44*a;* 12:13, 18; total, 10. Cases implying cause: 1:8; 2:6*a;* 4:1, 31*a;* 9:38*a;* total, 5. Cases implying concession: 3:13; 4:37*a;* 7:5, 21; 9:8*a;* total, 5. One case implying condition: 5:15.

SEC. 67. THE FACTS AS TO THE LOCATION AND FUNCTION OF THE GENITIVE ABSOLUTE IN ACTS, CHAPS. 13–28

Cases of the general adverbial: 13:42, 43*a;* 14:20*a;* 19:6, 33*a;* 20:7*a;* 21:5*b,* 40*a;* 25:7*d;* 26:14*a;* 27:2*c;* 28:9*a;* total, 12.

Cases implying time: 13:2*a,* 2*b,* 24; 16:16*a,* 35*a;* 17:16*a;* 18:12, 14, 27*a;* 20:9*c;* 21:10, 17, 31, 40*c;* 22:17*b;* 23:12*a,* 30*a;* 24:2, 10*a,* 20, 27*a;* 25:7*a,* 13*a,* 15*a,* 17*a,* 23*a,* 23*b,* 26; 26:10*b,* 24; 27:9*a,* 21*a,* 27; 28:3*a,* 3*b,* 6*a,* 6*b,* 13*b,* 17*b,* 25*b;* total, 40.

Cases implying cause: 15:2, 7*a;* 17:16*b;* 18:6*a,* 6*b;* 19:36*a,* 40*a;* 20:3*b;* 21:14*a,* 34; 22:23*a,* 23*b,* 23*c;* 23:7, 10*a;* 24:2*d,* 11*a,* 25*a;* 25:21, 23*c,* 25; 27:7*c,* 9*b,* 12*a,* 13*a,* 15*a,* 15*b,* 18, 20*a,* 20*b,* 30*a,* 30*b,* 30*c;* 28:19*a;* total, 34.

Cases implying concession: 18:20; 19:30. One case implying condition: 18:21*c.*

SEC. 68. SOME OBSERVATIONS ON THESE FACTS

As to the distribution of the cases of the genitive absolute in the Book of Acts, we notice that only 25 cases occur in chaps. 1–12, while 89 cases

occur in chaps. 13-28. It is to be observed that 22 cases in chaps. 13-28
are found in the last "We" passage, 27:1—28:16. The larger element
of narrative and the greater percentage of adverbial participles in chaps.
13-28 help to explain the large number of absolute genitives. The number in the book is 114, or nearly one-eleventh of all the participles in the
book.

As to the tenses in the genitive absolute, there are 63 cases of the present,
15 in chaps. 1-12, 48 in chaps. 13-28; 48 cases of the aorist, 8 in chaps.
1-12, 40 in chaps. 13-28, while only 3 cases of the perfect occur in the
book, 2 in the first portion, one in the second.

As to the relative frequency in the two portions of the book, we observe
that there occurs one participle to *ca.* 38½ lines in the first portion, while in
the second portion there occurs one to every 14$\frac{1}{4}$ lines. That is, there are
about two and three-fourths times as many absolute genitives to the page
in the second portion as there are in the first portion.

As to the significance of these absolute genitives in the Book of Acts,
most of them (50) imply time. Then comes the causal relation with
39 cases; general, 16; the concessive, 7; condition, 2. In chaps. 1-12
are found 10 temporal absolute genitives, 5 each, causal and concessive,
conditional, one. The implied relations of time and cause are much more
prominent in chaps. 13-28 than in chaps. 1-12 (there being 40 cases of
time and 34 cases of cause).

SEC. 69. SOME IRREGULARITIES IN THE GENITIVE ABSOLUTE IN THE BOOK OF ACTS

There are only a few loose constructions of the genitive absolute in the
Books of Acts. In 7:21 occurs the genitive absolute where the accusative
would have been the regular participial construction: "The daughter of
Pharaoh took him up after he had been cast out." But the genitive absolute, bringing in at the head of the sentence the casting-out of the little
child, makes more emphatic than the accusative could do the divine provi-
dence over the child in its concealment.

In 21:17 we have the genitive absolute where the accusative would be
regular, but the genitive absolute introducing the sentence and followed
by the accusative makes prominent the reception given to Paul and his
party when they arrived in Jerusalem. In 21:10, ἐπιμενόντων has no
substantive.

In 21:34 we find a genitive absolute which refers to the chiliarch of
vs. 33 who is the subject of the principal verb in vs. 34. Perhaps, this
loose genitive absolute adds a touch of vividness to the "inability" (μὴ

δυναμένου αὐτοῦ) of the chiliarch to find out the exact condition of affairs concerning Paul.

In 22:17 we find the genitive absolute, dative, and accusative referring to the same person. But there are three things to be made emphatic, Paul's return to Jerusalem, his praying, and his coming into an ecstasy, and no device of the author could have made more prominent each one of these things than the use of different cases. Perhaps, the necessity to change the tense of the participle (from aorist to present) made easier the change of cases (from dative to genitive absolute).

In 25:21 we have a genitive absolute and an accusative referring to the same person. There are a few other loose constructions of the genitive absolute in the book. But these few exceptions only emphasize the fact that the author of this book closely followed the rule to make the genitive absolute refer to a substantive not connected with the rest of the sentence.

CHAPTER VIII

THE FUNCTION OF THE TENSE IN THE PARTICIPLE IN THE BOOK OF ACTS

SEC. 70. GENERAL STATEMENT

Of the 1,283 participles in the Book of Acts 594 are in the present (231 in chaps. 1–12, 363 in chaps. 13–28); 588 are in the aorist (208 in chaps. 1–12, 380 in chaps. 13–28); 5 are in the future (one in chaps. 1–12, 4 in chaps. 13–28); 96 are in the perfect (38 in chaps. 1–12, 58 in chaps. 13–28).[1]

Tense in the indicative expresses the state and time of the action. In the subjunctive, optative, and infinitive, tense seems to refer almost exclusively to the state of the action, the time-relation being indicated only by the context or otherwise. Is the participle to be classed with the indicative, or with the subjunctive, optative, and infinitive, with respect to the time-function of its tenses? The facts of participial usage in the Book of Acts show that the chief function of tense in the participle is to denote the *state* of the action and that time is only implied from the context or some particle.

SEC. 71. FACTS IN THE BOOK OF ACTS BEARING ON THE PROBLEM OF TENSE-FUNCTION IN THE PARTICIPLE

THE PRESENT PARTICIPLE

The present participle generally refers to action simultaneous to that of the principal verb. Of the 594 cases in the Book of Acts 518 are used with reference to simultaneous action. All present participles not mentioned in the five subclasses below refer to simultaneous action.

Twenty-four present participles are used with reference to identical action, namely: 1:6; 3:25; 4:16a; 5:23, 27; 8:26a; 11:4; 14:11; 15:13; 16:28; 19:13c; 20:23; 21:21, 40; 22:26; 23:9, 12; 24:2, 9; 25:14; 26:31; 27:10, 33a; 28:26.

Thirty-nine present participles are used to express a general action (not limited as to time), namely: 1:12a, 20, 23; 3:2b, 11b; 6:9a; 7:58; 8:10b, 32; 9:11; 10:1, 2, 2, 2, 18b, 22, 22, 35, 35; 11:13; 12:10, 12b, 25; 13:1b, 16, 26, 43b; 15:18, 37; 16:14a; 17:24, 25, 25; 18:7b; 19:24, 26c; 27:8b, 14, 16.

Three present participles are used for a progressive action in the past, namely: 4:34a, 34b; 10:7a.

[1] The above figures count κείροντος (present) not κείραντος (aorist) in 8:32; and in 23:7, λαλοῦντος (present) not εἰπόντος (aorist).

Six present participles refer to future action, namely: 3:26 (purpose); 5:15 (equivalent to a more vivid future condition); 15:27 (purpose); 15:29 (more vivid future condition);[1] 18:21 (more vivid future condition); 19:4b; 21:3.

Four present participles refer to past action still in progress in the present, namely: 3:2a; 9:33; 24:10; 26:5.

THE AORIST PARTICIPLE

The aorist participle usually refers to action antecedent to that of the principal verb.   Of the 588 cases in the Book of Acts 540 refer to antecedent action.   All the aorist participles not mentioned in the two sub-classes below refer to antecedent action.[2]

Twenty-five aorist participles refer to identical action.   Εἰπών refers to identical action in 7:26, 27, 35, 40; 10:3; 11:13; 19:21; 21:14; 22:24; 24:22.   The remaining eight cases of εἰπών refer to antecedent action.[2] Ἀποκριθείς refers to identical action in 4:19; 5:29; 8:24, 34, 37; 19:15; 25:9.   The following cases of aorist participles from other verbs refer to identical action: 1:24; 5:30; 8:24; 9:25b; 10:33, 39; 13:22b; 21:1b.

Twenty-three aorist participles are doubtful as to their time-relation: 7:19, 26, 33; 9:12a, 12b; 10:3a, 3b; 11:12, 13, 13, 30; 12:4b; 15:9, 23; 16:6, 23b; 22:16b, 22:24; 23:24, 25, 35; 24:23; 26:13.[3]   In 25:13 the aorist participle seems to express purpose, i. e., to refer to the future.   But the text is probably corrupt as held by Hort in WH II, App., p. 100. The participle is very likely future.

THE FUTURE PARTICIPLE

All five of the cases of the future participle refer to a future action, four adverbials denoting purpose and one ascriptive describing what is to occur in the future.

THE PERFECT PARTICIPLE

The perfect participle usually refers to a past action and its resulting state.   In the Book of Acts the perfect participle of four verbs is used as a present participle, namely, of οἶδα, σύνοιδα, ἵστημι, παρίστημι, there being 3 cases of the first, 2 of the second, 9 of the third, and 2 of the fourth—16 in all.   In the other 80 cases the perfect participle refers to a past action and its resulting state.   Except in 2:13, "filled with new wine," the perfect seems to refer almost exclusively to the resulting state.

[1] 17:13a, 13b may be purpose and so future.

[2] ἀτενίσας refers apparently to simultaneous action in 3:4; 6:15; 7:55; 10:4; 11:6; 13:9; 14:9; 23:1.

[3] Several aorist participles refer to action begun in the past and continued into the present, e. g., 14:2, 11b, 20a, etc.

CHAPTER IX

A COMPLETE CLASSIFICATION OF THE PARTICIPLES IN THE BOOK OF ACTS

SEC. 72. PRELIMINARY STATEMENT

In this chapter we purpose to give a detailed classification of all the participles in the Book of Acts. Heretofore we have discussed merely the general classification—the three main classes, ascriptive, adverbial, and complementary. Here the subclasses of the three main divisions are given, so that the student interested may see at a glance where each participle belongs.

For details of the category adopted see Sec. 11. For the method of locating the participles see first paragraph, Sec. 62.

SEC. 73. THE ASCRIPTIVE PARTICIPLES IN ACTS, CHAPS. 1-12

RESTRICTIVE ATTRIBUTIVE

1:12a, 23; 2:2, 3b, 10, 22; 3:2a, 2b, 11b, 20; 4:12, 36a; 5:17b, 22a[1]; 6:9a; 7:26a, 58b; 8:10b, 26b; 9:7a, 11b, 22a, 32b; 10:2a, 7a, 17a, 18b; 11:1, 11, 13c, 19b, 22, 29; 12:10b, 12b, 25c; total, 36.

DESCRIPTIVE ATTRIBUTIVE

1:11b, 16a, 21; 2:23a; 4:11a, 11b, 14c; 5:7a; 6:3, 11a, 13a; 7:35b, 37, 38b, 38c; 8:12; 9:2b, 17b, 21d, 33a, 41c; 10:2b, 2c, 2d, 11c, 22a, 22b; 10:37a, 41; 11:3b, 5c, 21; 12:6b; total, 33.

PREDICATIVE ASCRIPTIVE

1:10a, 12b, 13, 14, 17; 2:3a, 5, 13b, 29, 42; 4:31b, 36b; 5:25b, 25c; 8:1, 9a, 9b, 13b, 16a, 16b, 28a, 28b; 9:9, 28a, 28b, 33b; 10:19b[2], 24a, 30; 11:5a; 12:5, 6a, 12c, 12d, 20a; total, 35.

SUBSTANTIVE ASCRIPTIVE

The most of these participles are equivalent to relative propositions.

1:3a, 16b, 19, 20; 2:7b, 9, 14b, 16[3], 41, 44, 47c; 3:2c, 10a[3], 10b; 4:4, 16b, 21c, 24b, 25, 32a, 32b, 34b; 5:5c, 7b, 9, 11, 14, 16b, 32; 6:9b[1], 15b; 7:10, 24c, 27a, 38a[3], 44, 52; 8:4a, 6, 7a, 7c, 32; 9:2a, 14, 21a, 21b[3], 21c, 35; 10:7c, 33b, 35a, 35b, 38c, 42a[3], 42b, 43, 44b; 11:19a, 28b[4]; 12:9b; total, 60.

[1] May be adverbial.
[2] Copula omitted.
[3] Also predicative.
[4] Participle in etymology used as pure substantive.

36

SEC. 74. ASCRIPTIVE PARTICIPLES IN ACTS, CHAPS. 13–28

RESTRICTIVE ATTRIBUTIVE

13:1*a*, 1*b*, 44[1]; 14:13*a*, 16; 15:22*b*, 37; 16:3*b*, 13*b*; 17:19*c*, 18:2*b*; 19:17; 20:9*a*, 19*b*; 21:2*b*, 26*b*, 38*a*, 38*b*; 22:12*b*, 25; 23:11*a*; 24:24*b*, 25*b*; 25:7*b*, 24*a*; 27:8*b*, 14, 16*b*, 28:11; total, 29.

DESCRIPTIVE ATTRIBUTIVE

13:27*c*, 32, 34, 43*b*, 50; 14:2, 3*b*, 15*b*, 15*c*; 15:16*a*, 18, 22*c*, 26; 16:4, 16*b*; 17:21, 26*b*; 18:7*b*[2], 24; 19:11, 13*a*, 16*c*, 24; 20:12, 22*a*, 32*a*; 21:8*c*, 23, 25*a*; 22:3*a*, 3*b*, 3*c*, 3*d*, 5*d*, 12*a*; 23:3*a*, 25*b*; 24:27*c*; 25:19; 26:4, 6*a*, 22*d*[3]; 27:2*b*, 6*b*, 12*c*, 39; 28:2*a*, 2*c*, 16; total, 49.

PREDICATIVE ASCRIPTIVE

13:11*a*, 48*b*; 14:7, 26; 16:9*a*, 9*b*, 9*c*, 12; 18:7*c*, 25*a*; 19:14, 32, 36*b*, 36*c*; 20:8, 9*b*[4], 13*c*; 21:3*c*, 9[5], 29, 33*b*; 22:19*a*, 19*b*, 20*a*, 20*b*, 20*c*, 29*c*; 25:10, 14*b*; 26:26*b*; total, 30.

SUBSTANTIVE ASCRIPTIVE

13:12*b*, 16*c*, 26, 27*a*, 29*a*[6], 31, 39, 40, 45*b*; 14:12; 15:5*a*, 16*b*, 19, 21*a*, 33*b*, 38*a*, 38*b*; 16:11*b*, 14*a*, 14*b*; 17:6*c*, 6*d*, 15*a*, 17*a*, 17*b*, 20, 24*a*, 31*a*[7]; 18:27*d*; 19:4*b*, 10, 12, 13*b*, 18*a*, 19*a*, 22*b*, 26*c*, 27[7], 37; 20:15*b*, 15*c*, 20, 22*b*, 30*b*, 32*b*, 34, 35*b*; 21:18, 20*b*, 28*b*; 22:5*c*, 9*a*, 9*b*, 11*b*, 19*c*, 20*d*, 29*a*; 23:2, 3*b*, 3*c*, 4, 13, 31*a*; 24:5*b*, 5*c*, 14*a*[8], 14*b*, 15, 25*d*; 25:16; 26:6*b*[8], 13*b*, 18, 22*b*[8], 29, 30; 27:11, 24*b*, 40*d*, 43*b*; 28:8*a*, 9*b*, 17*a*, 24, 30; total, 85.

SEC. 75. ADVERBIAL PARTICIPLES IN ACTS, CHAPS. 1–12

For particulars concerning the subclasses of adverbial participles see Sec. 11.

THE GENERAL ADVERBIAL PARTICIPLE

1:3*c*, 4*a*, 6*a*, 9*b*, 15; 2:14*a*, 46*a*, 46*b*, 47*a*, 47*b*; 3:4, 7, 8*a*, 11*a*, 26*a*; 4:7, 15, 18, 21*a*, 34*a*, 37*b*; 5:2*a*, 2*b*, 5*b*, 6*a*, 6*b*, 10*a*, 10*b*, 17*a*, 19, 20, 22*b*, 25*a*, 26, 27, 34, 40*a*, 40*b*; 6:2*a*, 2*b*, 6, 12; 7:4, 14, 19, 45, 57, 58*a*, 59*a*, 59*b*, 60*a*; 8:5, 7*b*, 15, 25*a*, 25*b*, 27*a*, 30*a*, 31, 35*a*, 35*b*, 40; 9:1*b*, 4*a*, 11*a*[9], 17*a*,

[1] Secondary reading, ἐχομένῳ (WH).
[2] May be regarded as substantive in apposition with Ἰούστου.
[3] Loose construction and uncertain as to use.
[4] Copula omitted.
[5] May be attributive.
[6] Reading somewhat doubtful (WH).
[7] Participle in etymology used as pure substantive.
[8] Possibly adverbial.
[9] Secondary reading (WH), but well attested (Tisch.).

18a, 18b, 25a, 26a, 27, 32a, 37a, 37b, 39a, 40a, 40b, 40c, 41a, 41b; 10:7b, 10, 13, 17b, 18a, 20a, 21, 23a, 23b, 24b, 25a, 25b, 27a, 34; 11:4a, 6, 7b, 20a, 23a, 28a, 30; 12:4a, 4b, 7a, 9a, 10a, 10c, 12a, 14b, 16b, 17a, 17b, 19c, 19d, 21a, 21b, 23, 25a, 25b; total, 119.

ADVERBIAL PARTICIPLES OF TIME

1:2, 9a, 10b, 22; 3:3a; 4:23; 5:4a[1], 4b, 21b, 23d; 6:1; 7:2, 12a, 26b, 30, 31b, 60b; 8:13a, 14; 9:1a, 39b, 39e, 40d; 10:8, 9a, 9b, 19a, 37b, 44a; 11: 26; 12:11, 13, 18; total, 33.

ADVERBIAL PARTICIPLES OF CAUSE

1:8[2], 18; 2:6a, 30a, 30b, 31a, 33a, 33b, 37; 3:5, 12a, 12b[3]; 4:1, 8, 13a, 13b, 14a, 21b, 24a, 31a; 5:5a, 21a, 33; 7:9, 24a, 31a, 32, 54, 55a; 8:13c, 18; 9:7b, 7c, 26b, 30, 38a, 38b; 10:29; 11:17, 18a, 23b; 12:3, 4c, 19a, 19b, 20b; total, 46.

ADVERBIAL PARTICIPLES OF MANNER OR MEANS

1:3b, 6b, 11a, 24; 2:7a, 12, 13a, 23b, 24, 40; 3:8b, 8c, 8d, 25; 4:2, 16a, 19; 5:16a, 23a, 28, 29, 30, 36, 41; 6:15a; 7:24d, 26c, 27b, 34[4], 35a, 36, 40, 55b; 8:3a, 3b, 4b, 10a, 10b, 19, 24, 26a, 34, 39; 9:8b, 22b, 25b, 29, 31a, 31b, 36, 38c, 39c, 39d; 10:4a, 4b, 20b, 26, 36[5], 38a, 38b, 39; 11:3a, 4b, 12, 18b, 19c, 20b; 12:7b; total, 68.

ADVERBIAL PARTICIPLES OF CONCESSION

3:13; 4:37a; 7:5, 21; 9:8a; 12:14a; total, 6.

ADVERBIAL PARTICIPLE OF CONDITION

5:15.

ADVERBIAL PARTICIPLES OF PURPOSE

3:26b; 8:27b; total, 2.

SEC. 76. ADVERBIAL PARTICIPLES IN ACTS, CHAPS. 13–28

GENERAL ADVERBIAL PARTICIPLES

13:5, 6, 7, 9b, 11b, 13a, 13b, 14a, 14b, 16a, 16b, 19, 22a, 29b, 42[6], 43a, 51; 14:9b, 13b, 19a, 19b, 20a, 20b, 21a, 21b, 23a, 23b, 24, 25, 27a, 27b; 15:1, 3a, 7b, 22a, 23, 25b, 30a, 30b, 33a, 36, 39, 40a, 40b; 16:3a, 7, 8, 9d, 11a, 13a, 15b, 17a, 18b, 19b, 20a, 22, 23a, 23b, 24, 25, 27d, 29a, 30, 33, 34a, 36, 37a, 37c, 39a, 39b, 40a; 17:1, 5b, 5c, 5d, 8, 9, 10, 15b, 19a, 22, 23a, 23b,

---

[1] May be condition (Winer).

[2] Time also.   [3] Supposed cause with ὡς.

[4] After the Septuagint which follows the Hebrew infinitive absolute.

[5] Secondary reading (WH), but well attested (Tisch.).

[6] Has a well-attested secondary reading (WH).

26a, 34[1]; 18:1, 6c, 7a, 8, 17, 18b, 18c[1], 19, 21a, 21b, 22a, 22b, 22c, 23a, 23b, 27b; 19:1, 5, 6, 8a, 9b, 16a, 19b, 21a, 21b, 22a, 25, 28a, 28b, 29, 31b, 33a, 33b, 34b[2], 35a; 20:1a, 1b, 1c, 2a, 2b, 5, 7a, 10a, 10b, 13a[3], 14, 15a, 17, 36b, 37; 21:2c, 3b, 4, 5a, 5b, 5c, 5d, 7b, 8a, 8b, 11a, 11b, 11c, 14b, 15, 19, 24a, 25b, 26a, 26d, 30, 32a[3], 33a, 40a, 40b; 22:10, 13a, 13b, 16a, 16b, 24, 26b, 27, 30b; 23:1, 9a, 10c, 11b, 12b, 14, 16b, 16c, 17, 18a, 18b, 19a, 19b, 22, 23, 25a, 27c, 30b, 31b, 32, 33a, 33b, 34a, 34b, 34c, 35; 24:23, 24a, 25c, 26b; 25:1, 3b, 5, 6b, 6c, 7d, 9c, 13b[3], 17b, 17c; 26:2a, 10a, 14a, 17, 21, 31a; 27:2a, 2c, 3b, 4, 5, 6a, 13c, 15c, 17a, 21b, 21c, 28a, 28b, 28c, 29b, 35a, 35b, 35c, 36, 40a, 40c, 41a, 41b; 28:2b, 5, 6d, 7, 8b, 8c, 8d, 9a, 12, 13a, 13b, 14, 15c, 18, 21, 23a; total, 254.

ADVERBIAL PARTICIPLES OF TIME

13:2a, 2b, 3a, 3b, 3c, 24, 36; 15:4, 31; 16:16a, 27a, 35a, 40b; 17:16a; 18:12, 14, 18a, 26, 27a, 27c; 19:2, 34a, 40b; 20:3a, 3c, 9c, 11a, 11b, 11c, 11d, 36a; 21:1a, 2a, 3a, 7a, 10, 17, 26c, 31, 37, 40c; 22:5a, 6a, 6b, 17a, 17b, 26a; 23:7[4], 12a, 16a, 30a; 24:2a, 10a, 20, 21, 25e, 27a; 25:6a, 7a, 12, 13a, 15a, 17a, 18, 23a, 23b, 26, 27; 26:10b, 12, 24; 27:9a, 12b, 21a, 27, 38a, 40b, 43c; 28:1, 3a, 3b, 3c, 6a, 10, 17b, 25b; total, 86.

ADVERBIAL PARTICIPLES OF CAUSE

13:4, 9a, 12a, 12c, 27b, 45a, 48a; 14:6, 9c, 11a, 14a, 17a, 19c; 15:2, 7a, 9[5], 25a, 32[6]; 16:6, 10, 18a, 19a, 20b[6], 21[6], 27b, 27e, 29b, 34b, 38; 17:5a, 6a, 16b, 24b, 25a[7], 25b, 29, 31b, 32; 18:2a, 6a, 6b, 25b; 19:31a, 36a, 40a[8]; 20:3b, 7b, 9d[8], 13b, 13d, 31a, 38; 21:14a, 20a, 27, 32b, 34; 22:2, 23a, 23b, 23c, 29b, 30a; 23:6, 10a, 10b, 15, 18c[6], 20, 27a, 27b, 27d, 28; 24:2c, 2d, 5a, 10c, 11a, 22a, 25a, 26a, 27b; 25:3a, 9a, 20, 21, 23c, 25; 26:2b, 3, 5, 11b, 22a; 27:3a, 7a, 7b, 7c, 9b, 12a, 13a, 13b, 15a, 15b, 17c, 18, 20a, 20b, 29a, 30a, 30b, 30c[7], 43a; 28:6b, 15a, 15b, 19a, 19b[7], 25a; total, 118.

ADVERBIAL PARTICIPLES OF MANNER OR MEANS

13:8, 15, 22b, 27d, 33, 43c, 45c, 46; 14:3a, 3c, 11b, 11c, 14b, 14c, 15a, 17b, 17c, 18, 22a, 22b; 15:3b, 5b, 8, 13, 21b, 24, 35a, 35b, 41; 16:15a, 16c, 17b, 28, 35b; 17:3a, 3b, 6b, 7, 11, 13a[9], 13b[9], 19b, 23c, 31c; 18:5, 11, 13, 23c, 28; 19:4a, 8b, 8c, 9a, 9c, 13c, 15, 16b, 18b, 18c, 26a, 26b, 28c; 20:19a, 21, 23, 26, 29[6], 30a[6], 35a; 21:1b, 13a, 13b, 16, 21, 24b, 28a, 36, 40d; 22:4a, 4b,

---

[1] Possibly cause.

[2] Loose construction. Some editors have κράζοντες.

[3] Doubtful reading (WH).

[4] εἰπόντος in the margin (WH).

[5] May be only general.

[6] Possibly ascriptive.

[7] Supposed cause with ὡς.

[8] Doubtful reading (WH).

[9] Probably purpose, too.

11*a*, 22, 26*c;* 23:9*b*, 12*c*, 21, 24; 24:2*b*, 8, 9, 22*b;* 25:7*c*, 9*b*, 14*a*, 15*b*, 24*b;* 26:7, 11*a*, 20, 22*c*, 26*a*, 31*b;* 27:8*a*, 10, 16*a*, 17*b*, 17*d*, 24*a*, 33*a*, 33*c*, 38*b*, 42; 28:23*b*, 23*c*, 26*a*, 26*b*, 31*a*, 31*b;* total, 118.

ADVERBIAL PARTICIPLES OF CONCESSION

13:28; 16:37*b;* 17:27, 30; 18:20, 25*c;* 19:30; 20:22*c;* 28:4*b*, 17*c;* total, 10.

ADVERBIAL PARTICIPLES OF CONDITION

15:29; 18:21*c;* total, 2.

ADVERBIAL PARTICIPLES OF PURPOSE

15:27; 22:5*b*, 24:11*b*, 17; total, 4.

SEC. 77. THE COMPLEMENTARY PARTICIPLES IN ACTS, CHAPS. 1–12[1]

SUBJECTIVE COMPLEMENTARY PARTICIPLES

5:42*a*, 42*b;* 6:13*b;* 10:33*a;* 12:16*a;* total, 5.

OBJECTIVE COMPLEMENTARY PARTICIPLES

1:11*c;* 2:6*b*, 11; 3:3*b*, 9*a*, 9*b;* 4:14*b;* 5:23*b*, 23*c;* 6:11*b*, 14; 7:12*b*[2], 24*b*, 55*c*, 56*a*, 56*b;* 8:13*d*, 23[2], 30*b;* 9:4*b*, 12*a*, 12*b;* 10:3*a*, 3*b*, 11*a*, 11*b*, 27*b*, 46*a*, 46*b;* 11:5*b*, 7*a*, 13*a*, 13*b;* total, 33.

SEC. 78. THE COMPLEMENTARY PARTICIPLES IN ACTS, CHAPS. 13–28

SUBJECTIVE COMPLEMENTARY PARTICIPLES

13:10; 20:31*b;* 21:32*c;* 27:33*b;* total, 4.

OBJECTIVE COMPLEMENTARY PARTICIPLES

14:9*a;* 15:12; 16:27*c;* 17:16*c*[2]; 19:35*b*[2]; 22:7, 18; 23:29*a*, 29*b;* 24:10*b*,[2] 12*a*, 12*b*, 18; 26:13*a*, 14*b;* 28:4*a*, 6*c*[2]; total, 17.

SEC. 79. AN ORDERLY PRESENTATION OF ALL THE PARTICIPLES IN THE BOOK OF ACTS

The following symbols are used to designate the classes and subclasses of participles. A * denotes ascriptive; *a*, attributive ascriptive; *p, predicative ascriptive; *s, substantive ascriptive. A † denotes adverbial; †g, general; †t, temporal; †c, causal; †m, manner or means; †cs, concessive; †co, conditional; †p, purpose. A ‡ denotes complementary; ‡s, subjective complementary; ‡o, objective complementary.

The participle is located in the verse by the same method as in the rest of this chapter.

1:2 †t, 3a *s, 3b †m, 3c †g, 4a †g, 6a †g, 6b †m, 8 †c, 9a †t, 9b †g, 10a *p,

---

[1] For the details as to the subclasses of the complementary participle see Sec. 11.

[2] In indirect discourse of which there are 6 cases in the Book of Acts.

10b †t, 11a †m, 11b *a, 11c ‡o, 12a *a, 12b *p, 13 *p, 14 *p, 15 †g, 16a *a, 16 b *s, 17 *p, 18 †c, 19 *s, 20 *s, 21 *a, 22 †t, 23 *a, 24 †m.

2:2 *a, 3a *p, 3b *a, 5 *p, 6a †c, 6b ‡o, 7a †m, 7b *s, 9 *s, 10 *a, 11 ‡o, 12 †m, 13a †m, 13b *p, 14a †g, 14b *s, 16 *s, 22 *a, 23b †m, 24 †m, 29 *p, 30a †c, 30b †c, 31 †c, 33a †c, 33b †c, 37 †c, 40 †m, 41 *s, 42 *p, 44 *s, 46a †g, 46b †g, 47a †g, 47b †g, 47c *s.

3:2a *a, 2b *a, 2c *s, 3a †t, 3b ‡o, 4 †g, 5 †c, 7 †g, 8a †g, 8b †m, 8c †m, 8d †m, 9a ‡o, 9b ‡o, 10a *s, 10b *s, 11a †g, 11b *a, 12a †c, 12b †c, 13 †cs, 20 *a, 25 †m, 26a †g, 26b †p.

4:1 †c, 2 †m, 4 *s, 7 †g, 8 †c, 11a *a, 11b *a, 12 *a, 13a †c, 13b †c, 14a †c, 14b ‡o, 14c *a, 15 †g, 16a †m, 16b *s, 18 †g, 19 †m, 21a †g, 21b †c, 21c *s, 23 †t, 24a †c, 24b *s, 25 *s, 31a †c, 31b *p, 32a *s, 32b *s, 34a †g, 34b *s, 36a *a, 36b *p, 37a †cs, 37b †g.

5:2a †g, 2b †g, 4a †t, 4b †t, 5a †c, 5b †g, 5c *s, 6a †g, 6b †g, 7a *a, 7b *s, 9 *s, 10a †g, 10b †g, 11 *s, 14 *s, 15 †co, 16a †m, 16b *s, 17a *g, 17b *a, 19 †g, 20 †g, 21a †c, 21b †t, 22a *a, 22b †g, 23a †m, 23b ‡o, 23c ‡o, 23d †t, 25a †g, 25b *p, 25c *p, 26 †g, 27 †g, 28 †m, 29 †m, 30 †m, 32 *s, 33 †c, 34 †g, 36 †m, 40a †g, 40b †g, 41 †m, 42a ‡s, 42b ‡s.

6:1 †t, 2a †g, 2b †g, 3 *a, 6 †g, 9a *a, 9b *s, 11a *a, 11b ‡o, 12 †g, 13a *a, 13b ‡s, 14 ‡o, 15a †m, 15b *s.

7:2 †t, 4 †g, 5 †cs, 9 †c, 10 *s, 12a †t, 12b ‡o, 14 †g, 19 †g, 21 †cs, 24a †c, 24b ‡o, 24c *s, 24d †m, 26a *a, 26b †t, 26c †m, 27a *s, 27b †m, 30 †t, 31a †c, 31b †t, 32 †c, 34 †m, 35a †m, 35b *a, 36 †m, 37 *a, 38a *s, 38b *a, 38c *a 40 †m, 44 *s, 45 †g, 52 *s, 54 †c, 55a †c, 55b †m, 55c ‡o, 56a ‡o, 56b ‡o, 57 †g, 58a †g, 58b *a, 59a †g, 59b †g, 60a †g, 60b †t.

8:1 *p, 3a †m, 3b †m, 4a *s, 4b †m, 5 †g, 6 *s, 7a *s, 7b †g, 7c *s, 9a *p, 9b *p, 10a †m, 10b †m, 12*a, 13a †t, 13b *p, 13c †c, 13d ‡o, 14 †t, 15 †g, 16a *p, 16b *p, 18 †c, 19 †m, 23‡o, 24 †m, 25a †g, 25b †g, 26a †m, 26b *a, 27a †g, 27b †p, 28a *p, 28b *p, 30a †g, 30b ‡o, 31 †g, 32 *s, 34 †m, 35a †g, 35b †g, 39 †m, 40 †g.

9:1a †t, 1b †g, 2a *s, 2b *a, 4a †g, 4b ‡o, 7a *a, 7b †c, 7c †c, 8a †cs, 8b †m, 9 *p, 11a †g, 11b *a, 12a ‡o, 12b ‡o, 14 *s, 17a †g, 17b *a, 18a †g, 18b †g, 21a *s, 21b *s, 21c *s, 21d *a, 22a *a, 22b †m, 25a †g, 25b †m, 26a †g, 26b †c, 27 †g, 28a *p, 28b *p, 29 †m, 30 †c, 31a †m, 31b †m, 32a †g, 32b *a, 33a *a, 33b *p, 35 *s, 36 †m, 37a †g, 37b †g, 38a †c, 38b †c, 38c †m, 39a †g, 39b †t, 39c †m, 39d †m, 39e †t, 40a †g, 40b †g, 40c †g, 40d †t, 41a †g, 41b †g, 41c *a.

10:2a *a, 2b *a, 2c *a, 2d *a, 3a ‡o, 3b ‡o, 4a †m, 4b †m, 7a *a, 7b †g, 7c *s, 8 †t, 9a †t, 9b †t, 10 †g, 11a ‡o, 11b ‡o, 11c *a, 13 †g, 17a *a, 17b †g, 18a †g, 18b *a, 19a †t, 19b *p, 20a †g, 20b †m, 21 †g, 22a *a, 22b *a, 23a †g,

23*b* †g, 24*a* *p, 24*b* †g, 25*a* †g, 25*b* †g, 26 †m, 27*a* †g, 27*b* ‡o, 29 †c, 30 *p, 33*a* ‡s, 33*b* *s, 34 †g, 35*a* *s, 35*b* *s, 36 †m, 37*a* *a, 37*b* †t, 38*a* †m, 38*b* †m, 38*c* *s, 39 †m, 41 *a, 42*a* *s, 42*b* *s, 43 *s, 44*a* †t, 44*b* *s, 46*a* ‡o, 46*b* ‡o.

11:1 *a, 3*a* †m, 3*b* *a, 4*a* †g, 4*b* †m, 5*a* *p, 5*b* ‡o, 5*c* *a, 6 †g, 7*a* ‡o, 7*b* †g, 11 *a, 12 †m, 13*a* ‡o, 13*b* ‡o, 13*c* *a, 17 †c, 18*a* †c, 18*b* †m, 19*a* *s, 19*b* *a, 19*c* †m, 20*a* †g, 20*b* †m, 21 *a, 22 *a, 23*a* †g, 23*b* †c, 26 †t, 28*a* †g, 28*b* *s, 29 *a, 30 †g.

12:3 †c, 4*a* †g, 4*b* †g, 4*c* †c, 5 *p, 6*a* *p, 6*b* *a, 7*a* †g, 7*b* †m, 9*a* †g, 9*b* *s, 10*a* †g, 10*b* *a, 10*c* †g, 11 †t, 12*a* †g, 12*b* *a, 12*c* *p, 12*d* *p, 13 †t, 14*a* †cs, 14*b* †g, 16*a* ‡s, 16*b* †g, 17*a* †g, 17*b* †g, 18 †t, 19*a* †c, 19*b* †c, 19*c* †g, 19*d* †g, 20*a* *p, 20*b* †c, 21*a* †g, 21*b* †g, 23 †g, 25*a* †g, 25*b* †g, 25*c* *a.

13:1*a* *a, 1*b* *a, 2*a* †t, 2*b* †t, 3*a* †t, 3*b* †t, 3*c* †t, 4 †c, 5 †g, 6 †g, 7 †g, 8 †m, 9*a* †c, 9*b* †g, 10 ‡s, 11*a* *p, 11*b* †g, 12*a* †c, 12*b* *s, 12*c* †c, 13*a* †g, 13*b* †g, 14*a* †g, 14*b* †g, 15 †m, 16*a* †g, 16*b* †g, 16*c* *s, 19 †g, 22*a* †g, 22*b* †m, 24 †t, 26 *s, 27*b* †c, 27*d* †m, 27*c* *a, 28 †cs, 29*a* *s, 29*b* †g, 31 *s, 32 *a, 33 †m, 34 *a, 36 †t, 39 *s, 40 *s, 42 †g, 43*a* †g, 43*b* *a, 43*c* †m, 44 *a, 45*a* †c, 45*b* *s, 45*c* †m, 46 †m, 48*a* †c, 48*b* *p, 50 *a, 51 †g.

14:2 *a, 3*a* †m, 3*b* *a, 3*c* †m, 6 †c, 7 *p, 9*a* ‡o, 9*b* †g, 9*c* †c, 11*a* †c, 11*b* †m, 11*c* †m, 12 *s, 13*a* *a, 13*b* †g, 14*a* †c, 14*b* †m, 14*c* †m, 15*a* †m, 15*b* *a, 15*c* *a, 16 *a, 17*a* †c, 17*b* †m, 17*c* †m, 18 †m, 19*a* †g, 19*b* †g, 19*c* †c, 20*a* †g, 20*b* †g, 21*a* †g, 21*b* †g, 22*a* †m, 22*b* †m, 23*a* †g, 23*b* †g, 24 †g, 25 †g, 26 *p, 27*a* †g, 27*b* †g.

15:1 †g, 2 †c, 3*a* †g, 3*b* †m, 4 †t, 5*a* *s, 5*b* †m, 7*a* †c, 7*b* †g, 8 †m, 9 †c, 12 ‡o, 13 †m, 16*a* *a, 16*b* *s, 18 *a, 19 *s, 21*a* *s, 21*b* †m, 22*a* †g, 22*b* *a, 22*c* *a, 23 †g, 24 †m, 25*a* †c, 25*b* †g, 26 *a, 27 †p, 29 †co, 30*a* †g, 30*b* †g, 31 †t, 32 †c, 33*a* †g, 33*b* *s, 35*a* †m, 35*b* †m, 36 †g, 37 *a, 38*a* *s, 38*b* *s, 39 †g, 40*a* †g, 40*b* †g, 41 †m.

16:3*a* †g, 3*b* *a, 4 *a, 6 †c, 7 †g, 8 †g, 9*a* *p, 9*b* *p, 9*c* *p, 9*d* †g, 10 †c, 11*a* †g, 11*b* *s, 12 *p, 13*a* †g, 13*b* *a, 14*a* *s, 14*b* *s, 15*a* †m, 15*b* †g, 16*a* †t, 16*b* *a, 16*c* †m, 17*a* †g, 17*b* †m, 18*a* †c, 18*b* †g, 19*a* †c, 19*b* †g, 20*a* †g, 20*b* †c, 21 †c, 22 †g, 23*a* †g, 23*b* †g, 24 †g, 25 †g, 27*a* †t, 27*b* †c, 27*c* ‡o, 27*d* †g, 27*e* †c, 28 †m, 29*a* †g, 29*b* †c, 30 †g, 33 †g, 34*a* †g, 34*b* †c, 35*a* †t, 35 *b* †m, 36 †g, 37*a* †g, 37*b* †cs, 37*c* †g, 38 †c, 39*a* †g, 39*b* †g, 40*a* †g, 40*b* †t.

17:1 †g, 3*a* †m, 3*b* †m, 5*a* †c, 5*b* †g, 5*c* †g, 5*d* †g, 6*a* †c, 6*b* †m, 6*c* *s, 6*d* *s, 7 †m, 8 †g, 9 †g, 10 †g, 11 †m, 13*a* †m, 13*b* †m, 15*a* *s, 15*b* †g, 16*a* †t, 16*b* †c, 16*c* ‡o, 17*a* *s, 17*b* *s, 19*a* †g, 19*b* †m, 19*c* *a, 20 *s, 21 *a, 22 †g, 23*a* †g, 23*b* †g, 23*c* †m, 24*a* *s, 24*b* †c, 25*a* †c, 25*b* †c, 26*a* †g, 26*b* *a, 27 †cs, 29 †c, 30 †cs, 31*a* *s, 31*b* †c, 31*c* †m, 32 †c, 34 †g.

18:1 †g, 2*a* †c, 2*b* *a, 5 †m, 6*a* †c, 6*b* †c, 6*c* †g, 7*a* †g, 7*b* *a, 7*c* *p, 8 †g, 11 †m, 12 †t, 13 †m, 14 †t, 17 †g, 18*a* †t, 18*b* †g, 18*c* †g, 19 †g, 20 †cs,

21a †g, 21b †g, 21c †co, 22a †g, 22b †g, 22c †g, 23a †g, 23b †g, 23c †m,
24 *a, 25a *p, 25b †c, 25c †cs, 26 †t, 27a †t, 27b †g, 27c †t, 27d *s, 28 †m.

19:1 †g, 2 †t, 4a †m, 4b *s, 5 †g, 6 †g, 8a †g, 8b †m, 8c †m, 9a †m,
9b †g, 9c †m, 10 *s, 11 *a, 12 *s, 13a *a, 13b *s, 13c †m, 14 *p, 15 †m,
16a †g, 16b †m, 16c *a, 17 *a, 18a *s, 18b †m, 18c †m, 19a *s, 19b †g, 21a †g,
21b †g, 22a †g, 22b *s, 24 *a, 25 †g, 26a †m, 26b †m, 26c *s, 27 *s, 28a †g,
28b †g, 28c †m, 29 †g, 30 †cs, 31a †c, 31b †g, 32 *p, 33a †g, 33b †g, 34a †t,
34b †g, 35a †g, 35b ‡o, 36a †c, 36b *p, 36c *p, 37 *s, 40a †c, 40b †t.

20:1a †g, 1b †g, 1c †g, 2a †g, 2b †g, 3a †t, 3b †c, 3c †t, 5 †g, 7a †g, 7b †c,
8 *p, 9a *a, 9b *p, 9c †t, 9d †c, 10a †g, 10b †g, 11a †t, 11b †t, 11c †t, 11d †t,
12 *a, 13a †g, 13b †c, 13c *p, 13d †c, 14 †g, 15a †g, 15b *s, 15c *s, 17 †g,
19a †m, 19b *a, 20 *s, 21 †m, 22a *a, 22b *s, 22c †cs, 23 †m, 26 †m, 29 †m,
30a †m, 30b *s, 31a †c, 31b ‡s, 32a *a, 32b *s, 34 *s, 35a †m, 35b *s, 36a †t,
36b †g, 37 †g, 38 †c.

21:1a †t, 1b †m, 2a †t, 2b *a, 2c †g, 3a †t, 3b †g, 3c *p, 4 †g, 5a †g,
5b †g, 5c †g, 5d †g, 7a †t, 7b †g, 8a †g, 8b †g, 8c *a, 9 *p, 10 †t, 11a †g,
11b †g, 11c †g, 13a †m, 13b †m, 14a †c, 14b †g, 15 †g, 16 †m, 17 †t, 18 *s,
19 †g, 20a †c, 20b *s, 21 †m, 23 *a, 24a †g, 24b †m, 25a *a, 25b †g, 26a †g,
26b *a, 26c †t, 26d †g, 27 †c, 28a †m, 28b *s, 29 *p, 30 †g, 31 †t, 32a †g,
32b †c, 32c ‡s, 33a †g, 33b *p, 34 †c, 36 †m, 37 †t, 38a *a, 38b *a, 40a †g,
40b †g, 40c †t, 40d †m.

22:2 †c, 3a *a, 3b *a, 3c *a, 3d *a, 4a †m, 4b †m, 5a †t, 5b †p, 5c *s,
5d *a, 6a †t, 6b †t, 7 ‡o, 9a *s, 9b *s, 10 †g, 11a †m, 11b *s, 12a *a, 12b *a,
13a †g, 13b †g, 16a †g, 16b †g, 17a †t, 17b †t, 18 ‡o, 19a *p, 19b *p, 19c *s,
20a *p, 20b *p, 20c *p, 20d *s, 22 †m, 23a †c, 23b †c, 23c †c, 24 †g, 25 *a,
26a †t, 26b †g, 26c †m, 27 †g, 29a *s, 29b †c, 29c *p, 30a †c, 30b †g.

23:1 †g, 2 *s, 3a *a, 3b *s, 3c *s, 4 *s, 6 †c, 7 †t, 9a †g, 9b †m, 10a †c,
10b †c, 10c †g, 11a *a, 11b †g, 12a †t, 12b †g, 12c †m, 13 *s, 14 †g, 15 †c,
16a †t, 16b †g, 16c †g, 17 †g, 18a †g, 18b †g, 18c †c, 19a †g, 19b †g, 20 †c,
21 †m, 22 †g, 23 †g, 24 †m, 25a †g, 25b *a, 27a †c, 27b †c, 27c †g, 27d †c,
28 †c, 29a ‡o, 29b ‡o, 30a †t, 30b †g, 31a *s, 31b †g, 32 †g, 33a †g, 33b †g,
34a †g, 34b †g, 34c †g, 35 †g.

24:2a †t, 2b †m, 2c †c, 2d †c, 5a †c, 5b *s, 5c *s, 8 †m, 9 †m, 10a †t,
10b ‡o, 10c †c, 11a †c, 11b †p, 12a ‡o, 12b ‡o, 14a *s, 14b *s, 15 *s, 17 †p,
18 ‡o, 20 †t, 21 †t, 22a †c, 22b †m, 23 †g, 24a †g, 24b *a, 25a †c, 25b *a,
25c †g, 25d *s, 25e †t, 26a †c, 26b †g, 27a †t, 27b †c, 27c *a.

25:1 †g, 3a †c, 3b †g, 5 †g, 6a †t, 6b †g, 6c †g, 7a †t, 7b *a, 7c †m, 7d †g,
9a †c, 9b †m, 9c †g, 10 *p, 12 †t, 13a †t, 13b †g, 14a †m, 14b *p, 15a †t,
15b †m, 16 *s, 17a †t, 17b †g, 17c †g, 18 †t, 19 *a, 20 †c, 21 †c, 23a †t, 23b †t,
23c †c, 24a *a, 24b †m, 25 †c, 26 †t, 27 †t.

26:2a †g, 2b †c, 3 †c, 4 *a, 5 †c, 6a *a, 6b *s, 7 †m, 10a †g, 10b †t, 11a †m,
11b †c, 12 †t, 13a ‡o, 13b *s, 14a †g, 14b ‡o, 17 †g, 18 *s, 20 †m, 21 †g,
22a †c, 22b *s, 22c †m, 22d *a, 24 †t, 26a †m, 26b *p, 29 *s, 30 *s, 31a †g,
31b †m.

27:2a †g, 2b *a, 2c †g, 3a †c, 3b †g, 4 †g, 5 †g, 6a †g, 6b *a, 7a †c, 7b †c,
7c †c, 8a †m, 8b *a, 9a †t, 9b †c, 10 †m, 11 *s, 12a †c, 12b †t, 12c *a,
13a †c, 13b †c, 13c †g, 14 *a, 15a †c, 15b †c, 15c †g, 16a †m, 16b *a, 17a †g,
17b †m, 17c †c, 17d †m, 18 †c, 20a †c, 20b †c, 21a †t, 21b †g, 21c †g, 24a †m,
24b *s, 27 †t, 28a †g, 28b †g, 28c †g, 29a †c, 29b †g, 30a †c, 30b †c, 30c †c,
33a †m, 33b ‡s, 33c †m, 35a †g, 35b †g, 35c †g, 36 †g, 38a †t, 38b †m, 39 *a,
40a †g, 40b †t, 40c †g, 40d *s, 41a †g, 41b †g, 42 †m, 43a †c, 43b *s, 43c †t.

28:1 †t, 2a *a, 2b †g, 2c *a, 3a †t, 3b †t, 3c †t, 4a ‡o, 4b †cs, 5 †g, 6a †t,
6b †c, 6c ‡o, 6d †g, 7 †g, 8a *s, 8b †g, 8c †g, 8d †g, 9a †g, 9b *s, 10 †t,
11 *a, 12 †g, 13a †g, 13b †g, 14 †g, 15a †c, 15b †c, 15c †g, 16* a, 17a *s,
17b †t, 17c †cs, 18 †g, 19a †c, 19b †c, 21 †g, 23a †g, 23b †m, 23c †m, 24 *s,
25a †c, 25b †t, 26a †m, 26b †m, 30 *s, 31a †m, 31 b †m.

PART II

INFERENCES FROM THE FACTS CONCERNING THE PARTICIPLE IN THE BOOK OF ACTS

CHAPTER X

THE NATURE OF THE GREEK IN THE BOOK OF ACTS

SEC. 80. PRELIMINARY STATEMENT

It now remains to synthesize the accumulated facts of Part I and see to what conclusions they naturally lead. There are five problems connected with the Book of Acts on which the participle throws more or less light—the nature of its Greek, its sources, its unity, its authorship, and the composition of its addresses.

What bearing, then, have the facts of Part I on the nature of the Greek in which the Book of Acts was wrtiten?

SEC. 81. THE GREEK OF THE BOOK OF ACTS COMPARED WITH
THAT OF THE CLASSICAL PERIOD

Take Thucydides, Herodotus, Xenophon, Plato, and Demosthenes as representative authors of this period. We find (p. 10, Part I) that Thucydides averages 13 participles per page;[1] Herodotus, $17\frac{1}{2}$; Xenophon, $12\frac{2}{3}$; Plato, $10\frac{1}{8}$; and Demosthenes, $10\frac{3}{4}$. The average ranges from $10\frac{1}{8}$ to $17\frac{1}{2}$, the general average for these classical authors being *ca.* $12\frac{4}{5}$.' The Book of Acts has an average of *ca.* $17\frac{1}{4}$ per page. That is, *ca.* 40 per cent. more participles are found in the Book of Acts than occur in the great classical authors. But it is to be observed, the preponderance of narrative in the Book of Acts helps to account for this higher average.

If we compare the nature of the participles in the Book of Acts with that of the classical authors, we find that the ascriptive participle in classical Greek ranges from $22\frac{2}{3}$ per cent. (in Thucydides) to $45\frac{1}{7}$ (in Plato), giving an average of *ca.* $27\frac{1}{2}$ per cent. The Book of Acts has $28\frac{1}{4}$ per cent. ascriptive—a little greater percentage than that of Thucydides or Herodotus, a little less than that of Plato or Demosthenes, but about the same as that of Xenophon. The adverbials in the classical authors range from $50\frac{1}{7}$ per cent. (Plato) to $72\frac{1}{3}$ (Thucydides), giving a general average of *ca.* 62 per cent. The Book of Acts has nearly 68 per cent. adverbials—a little more

---

[1] Page means 30 lines throughout this treatise.

45

than Xenophon, a little less than Thucydides or Herodotus, but considerably more than Plato or Demosthenes (probably because Acts contains more narrative). The complementary participle in the classical
authors ranges from $4\frac{5}{8}$ per cent. (Plato) to $11\frac{1}{4}$ per cent. (Demosthenes),
averaging for classical Greek *ca.* $6\frac{3}{4}$ per cent. The Book of Acts has *ca.*
4 per cent. complementary.

Thus we see the Book of Acts surpasses in frequency of participles the
general average of the classical authors and is excelled by only one,
Herodotus (only by a fraction of 1 per cent.). In its proportion of
ascriptive, adverbial, and complementary participles the Book of Acts
comes fairly near to the general average found in the classical authors,
except that in its complementary participle it falls below the lowest
average (that of Plato).

SEC. 82.   THE GREEK OF THE BOOK OF ACTS COMPARED WITH THAT OF THE LITERARY κοινή

Polybius averages $17\frac{4}{8}$ per page; Strabo, $13\frac{1}{2}$; Plutarch, 14, while
Josephus runs up to 20, giving an average for the literary κοινή of nearly
$16\frac{1}{2}$ (Acts being $17\frac{1}{8}$).

Polybius has $27\frac{4}{8}$ per cent. ascriptive; Strabo, $46\frac{4}{8}$ per cent.; Josephus,
$16\frac{4}{8}$ per cent.; Plutarch, 29 per cent., a general average of 30 per cent.
(Acts having $28\frac{1}{4}$ per cent.). Polybius has $69\frac{4}{8}$ per cent. adverbial; Strabo,
$51\frac{1}{2}$; Plutarch, $65\frac{1}{4}$, while Josephus reaches 78 per cent., a general average
of nearly 66 (Acts having nearly 68 per cent.). The complementary par-
ticiple is less frequent in the literary κοινή than in classical Greek, ranging
from $1\frac{9}{10}$ (Strabo) to $5\frac{3}{4}$ (Plutarch). Josephus has nearly as many as
Plutarch, $5\frac{1}{2}$ per cent., but Polybius has only $2\frac{1}{2}$ per cent. The average for
the literary κοινή is $3\frac{4}{8}$ per cent. (Acts less than 4 per cent.).

Thus we see, the participles of the Book of Acts, as to frequency, show
about the same Greek that we find in literary κοινή. At any rate, the Greek
of the Book of Acts is more like that of the literary κοινή than that of the
classical authors. As to the proportion of the three classes of participles,
the Book of Acts has just a few less ascriptives and just a few more
adverbials than the average in the literary κοινή, the complementary
participle being of about the same frequency in both. The Book
of Acts is more like the literary κοινή than classical Greek in the per-
centage of its ascriptives (proportion, $28\frac{1}{4}$ in Acts; $27\frac{1}{2}$ in literary κοινή; 33
in classical). In the percentage of its adverbials, likewise, the Book of Acts
is closer to the literary κοινή than to the classical Greek (proportion, Acts,
68; literary κοινή, 66; classical, 62). There is a still greater difference in

complementary participles (Acts, 4 per cent.; literary *κοινή*, $3\frac{4}{5}$; classical, $6\frac{3}{4}$) between the Book of Acts and classical Greek, on the one hand, and the Book of Acts and literary *κοινή*, on the other hand.

SEC. 83. THE GREEK OF THE BOOK OF ACTS COMPARED WITH THE GREEK OF THE PAPYRI AND THE SEPTUAGINT

From p. 10 we find that the participles in the Septuagint average only $6\frac{1}{2}$ per page, in the papyri, a little over $6\frac{4}{5}$. The Septuagint has 79 per cent. ascriptive; $19\frac{1}{3}$ per cent. adverbial; $1\frac{2}{3}$ per cent. complementary. The papyri have $84\frac{1}{4}$ per cent. ascriptive; 14 per cent. adverbial; $2\frac{3}{4}$ per cent. complementary. The Book of Acts averages $17\frac{1}{6}$, with $28\frac{1}{4}$ per cent. ascriptive; nearly 68 per cent. adverbial; *ca.* 4 per cent. complementary. Thus we see that the Greek of the Book of Acts differs much from the Greek of the Septuagint and the vernacular papyri. Indeed, the Greek of the Book of Acts is upon an average better than the common dialect Greek, which we find in the Septuagint and the papyri.

SEC. 84. THE GREEK OF THE BOOK OF ACTS COMPARED WITH THAT OF OTHER BOOKS OF THE NEW TESTAMENT

See p. 23 for the facts. As compared with the Greek of Paul in three of his great epistles (Galatians, I Corinthians, Romans), we notice that Paul averages *ca.* 9 participles per page, $73\frac{1}{2}$ per cent. ascriptive; $25\frac{2}{3}$ per cent. adverbial; less than 1 per cent. complementary. Thus we see that Paul's Greek is much more like the vernacular *κοινή* of the Septuagint and the papyri than that of the Book of Acts or of the literary *κοινή*. But, observe, Paul's lack of narrative helps to account for this difference.

The Epistle to the Hebrews averages 14 per page, 57 per cent. ascriptive; 41 per cent. adverbial; 2 per cent. complementary. In frequency of participles the Greek of Hebrews is nearer to the classical Greek than to the literary or vernacular *κοινή*; it is also nearer to the classical Greek than it is to that of the Book of Acts. When we consider the nature of the participle, we observe that the Epistle to the Hebrews contains a much smaller percentage of ascriptives and a much larger proportion of adverbials than the vernacular *κοινή*, and yet the percentage of ascriptives in Hebrews is much larger than in the Book of Acts, while that of the adverbials is much smaller (the proportion of ascriptives being 57 to $28\frac{1}{4}$, nearly double; that of adverbials, 41 to 68, over a third less). Therefore, we conclude, there is a wide difference between the Greek of the Book of Acts and that of Hebrews, while there is not so great a difference between classical Greek and that of Hebrews. Likewise, the Greek of the Book of Acts is nearer to that of the literary κοινή than it is to the Greek of Hebrews (cf. figures on pp. 10 and 23).

The Johannine writings show a Greek more in accord with that of the vernacular κοινή than with that of the literary κοινή (the First Epistle more so than the gospel, the epistle not containing a single adverbial participle but 94¼ per cent. ascriptive). As to Matthew and Mark, their frequency of participles is nearly the same as that of classical Greek, much less than that of the literary κοινή, while much greater than that of the vernacular. Strange as it may seem, the Greek of Mark, as seen from its participial side, is nearer to that of the literary κοινή than Matthew is. (But the discourses in Matthew help to account for this.) Stranger still, the Greek of Mark is more like that of the Book of Acts and the literary κοινή than it is like the vernacular (see pp. 10 and 23).

The Greek of First Peter is more akin to that of the vernacular than it is to the literary κοινή (except that the participle is much more frequent in First Peter than in the vernacular, but not so frequent as in the literary κοινή).

SEC. 85. GENERAL CONCLUSIONS

First, the Greek of the Book of Acts is not so near to the classical usage as is the letter to the Hebrews, but it is more like that of the literary κοινή than that of Hebrews is.

Secondly, the Greek of the Book of Acts is less like that of the vernacular κοινή than that of Paul.

Thirdly, the Greek of the Book of Acts is still more superior, from the literary point of view, to that of the Johannine writings, but not so much superior in literary merit to the Greek of Matthew and Mark (we compare the Greek of the Third Gospel in a subsequent chapter).

Of course, all these conclusions as to the nature of the Greek of the Book of Acts as compared with that of other books of the New Testament, with that of the classical, literary, or vernacular κοινή, are based exclusively on the participial usage. Other features of style might modify these conclusions. We shall see in the next chapters that the nature of the Greek in the Book of Acts varies in different portions of the book.

CHAPTER XI

THE UNITY OF THE BOOK OF ACTS SEEN IN THE LIGHT OF THE PARTICIPLE

SEC. 86. OPENING STATEMENT

The traditional school has ever contended for the unity of the book. Not even the Tübingen school gave any serious attention to the discussion of the unity of the Book of Acts. With them the *Tendenz* (tendency) was the main thing in the book. It was not till Spitta published in 1891 his *Die Apostelgeschichte, ihre Quellen*, etc., on the sources of the Book of Acts that the question of unity was seriously discussed. Spitta claims that the book is the work of a redactor based on two parallel sources, A and B, each beginning with the ascension of Jesus and both continuing throughout the Book of Acts. J. Weiss, in the main, accepts Spitta's view as to the lack of unity in the book.

Carl Clemen more recently has regarded the Book of Acts as the production of two redactors, Rj friendly, Ra hostile, to the Jews, the former using as a source HPe (History of Peter), the latter using as a source HPa (History of Paul).

Jülicher denies that there are three authors to the book, a Judaist, an Anti-Judaist, and a Neutral (as claimed by some). He thinks that the book comes from one pen (but not Luke's).

Still more recently Harnack (*Lukas der Arzt*, etc., especially pp. 96–99, 122–37) argues, from lexical and stylistic facts, for the unity of the book, claiming that, not only chaps. 1–12 and 13–28 come from the same hand, but also that the author of the whole book is none other than the author of the "We" passages. What light does the participial usage in the Book of Acts throw on this question?

SEC. 87. THE PARTICIPIAL USAGE IN THE TWO MAIN PORTIONS

The participles in Pe (chaps. 1–12) average $15\frac{1}{8}$; in Pa (chaps. 13–28) they average 19. Pe has $34\frac{7}{12}$ per cent. ascriptive, Pa has *ca.* 24 per cent. ascriptive. Pe has $57\frac{7}{8}$ per cent. adverbial, Pa has $73\frac{1}{2}$ per cent. adverbial. Pe has $7\frac{3}{4}$ per cent. complementary, while Pa has only $2\frac{1}{2}$ per cent. complementary. So we see that the author of Pe has nearly 25 per cent. higher average than Pa, and used nearly one-third more ascriptive participles than the author of Pa.

Furthermore (pp. 28, 29) we saw that the author of Pe used a much larger percentage of periphrastic, or predicative, ascriptives than did the author of Pa—there being one periphrastic participle to every 26⅔ lines in Pe, but only one to *ca.* 44 lines in Pa.

What is the significance of these facts? Do they mean that the same author could not have written the two portions, Pe and Pa, with so different usage in each as to ascriptive participles? Before drawing any conclusion we must consider if it is not possible for the same writer in the same production to differ as much as this in his use of ascriptive participles. Take as an example Paul, in Rom., chaps. 9–11 and 12–14. In the former section occur only 24 ascriptive participles to 168 lines, one to *ca.* 7 lines; in the latter section occur 52 to 141 lines, a little over one to 3 lines. That is, Paul uses over twice as many ascriptives in chaps. 12–14 as he does in chaps. 9–11—a much greater difference than we find in Pe and Pa.

Why so great a difference in the percentage of ascriptives in Rom., chaps. 9–11 and 12–14? Is it not due primarily to the different nature of the two sections? Chaps. 9–11 give an argument closely thought out; chaps. 12–14, an exhortation which includes a great deal of descriptive matter (especially chap. 12 on the various classes). In argumentation an author naturally uses the finite verb with particles instead of participles, while in exhortation it is natural to use more ascriptives. Moreover, in chaps. 9–11 occurs much quoted matter in which are found very few participles.

Does the different nature of Pe and Pa warrant the difference of 30 per cent. in the proportion of ascriptives in each? There is not much difference between the nature of Pe and Pa, except that Pe contains more speeches (some long) and less narrative, also breathes a more Hebraistic atmosphere, which facts, perhaps, help to explain the larger proportion of ascriptives.

What can be said of the adverbials in Pe and Pa? In Pa there are about 30 per cent. more adverbials than in Pe. The three reasons mentioned above help to explain the increased percentage of adverbials in Pa. The purer the narrative and the less Hebraistic the writing (other things being equal) the more adverbials will be used.

The use of the complementary participle is so different in Pe and Pa as to cast some doubt upon the unity of the book, there being about three times as many in Pe as in Pa. Nor can we claim that the Hebraistic tone of Pe helps to explain the difference, since the complementary participle is seldom used in the Septuagint of Exodus, Deuteronomy, and Judges (1⅘ per cent.). Homer and the author of Pe use about the same percentage of complementary participles, while Polybius and the author of Pa use the same number. Upon the whole we may say, the participial usage is not strongly for the unity of the two main portions of the book, though the different tone and different nature of the two portions, not different authorship, may explain the different participial usage.

SEC. 88.   THE PARTICIPIAL USAGE IN THE SUBDIVISIONS OF CHAPS. 1–12

These chapters easily fall into the following sections: 1:1–14; 1:15–26; chap. 2; chaps. 3–5; 6:1–7; 6:8—7:60; chap. 8; 9:1–31; 9:32—11:18; 11:19–26; 11:27—12:25.

Let us bear in mind that the participles in Pe average $15\frac{1}{8}$, $34\frac{7}{12}$ per cent. ascriptive, $57\frac{7}{8}$ per cent. adverbial, $7\frac{3}{4}$ per cent. complementary. Now if one author composed the whole of Pe, we may expect the sections to agree fairly well, in participial usage, with one another and with the general average of Pe.   They need not agree exactly, for different participial usage may be due to different sources, different tone and nature of the section, not to different authorship.

1:1–14 (ascension of Jesus and the stay of the disciples in the upper room) has 19 participles, an average of $13\frac{1}{2}$ per page, *ca.* 36 per cent. ascriptive, *ca.* 58 per cent. adverbial, *ca.* 5 per cent. complementary.   By comparison we notice that the participial usage of this section closely resembles that of Pe as a whole.

1:15–26 (election of Matthias) contains 11 participles, an average of 12 + per page, over 63 per cent. ascriptive, 37 − per cent. adverbial.   This participial usage is radically different from that of Pe, and would suggest a different hand, were it not that a large part of this section is an address. Hence, this section can furnish proof neither for nor against the unity of Pe. The author may be influenced by a Hebraistic source, since the ascriptive participle prevails in the section.

Chap. 2 (Pentecost and its immediate results) has 37 participles, an average of $10\frac{1}{4}$ per page, the ascriptive and adverbial each $47\frac{1}{4}$ per cent., *ca.* $5\frac{1}{2}$ per cent. complementary.   Three things must be considered in estimating the participial usage of this section: its large amount of quoted matter, its general Hebraistic tone (dealing with intensely Jewish matters), and the fact that it is not all narrative.   Hence, we find the ascriptive participles above the average for Pe, but the adverbial and complementary participles below its average.   This difference does not necessarily indicate a different author, since the nature of the section largely explains the participial usage on the basis of unity of authorship.

Chaps. 3–5 (early history of the Jerusalem church) contain 112 participles, an average of *ca.* $14\frac{1}{2}$, *ca.* 35 per cent. ascriptive, *ca.* 58 per cent. adverbial, *ca.* 7 per cent. complementary.   These figures show a remarkably similar style in this section to that of Pe.

6:1–7 (internal trouble leading to the election of the Seven) has only five participles, an average of less than 10 per page, 20 per cent. ascriptive and 80 per cent. adverbial. That is, this section has very little Hebraistic tone, but seems to be a free composition unhampered by the style of a written source. The writer of this section writes like a κοινή writer unfettered by Judaistic influences. Of course any writer might write this number of lines without using a complementary participle. The participial usage of this section agrees more closely with that of Pa than that of Pe.

6:8—7:60 (the Stephen section) contains 56 participles, an average of *ca.* 10 per page, 34 per cent. ascriptive, *ca.* 52½ per cent. adverbial, *ca.* 13½ per cent. complementary, the number of ascriptives being about the same as that of Pe, the number of adverbials a little less, and the number of complementary participles being nearly double. The number of adverbials is, doubtless, cut down by the large percentage of quoted matter in Stephen's address. The large number of complementary participles is difficult to explain. If, in this section, the usage of its ascriptive and adverbial participles did not so closely harmonize with that of Pe, we might conclude that the excessive use of complementary participles suggested another hand.

Chap. 8 (the Philip section) contains 45 participles, an average of 15½, 32½ per cent. ascriptive, *ca.* 63 per cent. adverbial, *ca.* 4 per cent. complementary. These figures are fairly close to those of Pe, the difference being more adverbial and less complementary participles. This Philip section has only one quotation, and in its original portion fairly represents the author of Pe in his participial usage.

9:1–31 (Saul's conversion and early Christian activity) contains 37 participles (38 if ἀναστάς in v. 11 be included), an average of *ca.* 16⅘, nearly 38 per cent. ascriptive, a little over 54 per cent. adverbial, *ca.* 8 per cent. complementary. This section has a participial usage similar to that of Pe, except the slightly increased average and a greater percentage of ascriptive and complementary participles. The increase of the latter is due to the vision described.

9:32—11:18 (Peter's missionary work) contains 103 participles, an average of 19¼ per page, 32⅔ per cent. ascriptive, 54¼ per cent. adverbial, *ca.* 12½ per cent. complementary. Two things are remarkable in this section, the high average and the large number of complementary participles. The ascriptive and adverbial participles are just a little below the average for Pe.

Is there any explanation (besides different authorship, or editorial work) for this excessive average—*ca.* 25 per cent. greater than that of Pe?

The preponderating narrative element helps to account for the large average; the visions of Peter and Cornelius (the former twice told) increase the number of complementary participles; also written sources might have led the same author to use more participles than was his usual habit. Yet, if there were sufficiently weighty arguments from other directions pointing to a different author for this section, the participial usage might lend its evidence for different authorship.

11:19–26 (the gospel reaches Antioch) has 10 participles, an average of 16⅔ per page, 40 per cent. ascriptive and 60 per cent. adverbial. The section is not radically different from Pe in participial usage, except it has no complementary participle. Yet, the section is too short for us to base conclusions on it for or against the unity of Pe.

11:27—12:25 (the Jerusalem church and Herod Agrippa I) contains 43 participles, an average of 19½ per page, *ca.* 28 per cent. ascriptive, 69½ per cent. adverbial, less than 2½ per cent. complementary. These figures show three irregularities: excessive average, a small number of ascriptives with a large number of adverbials, and a very small number of complementary participles. How explain this variant usage? Either by the preponderating narrative of the section and the source as containing a large number of participles, or by the hypothesis of a different author. Since the first condition is present and the second condition may be present, it is not necessary to suppose a different author to account for the variant usage of participles in this section.

SEC. 89. TABLE ILLUSTRATING THE SUBSECTIONS OF PE

Section	Average per Page of 30 Lines	Ascriptive Per cent.	Adverbial Per cent.	Complementary Per cent.
1:1–14	13½	36	58	*ca.* 5
1:15–26	12+	63	37	...
Chap. 2	10¼	47¼	47¼	5½
Chaps. 3–5	14⅔	35	58	7
6:1–7	10–	20	80	...
6:8—7:60	10	34	52½	13½
Chap. 8	15½	32½	63	4+
9:1–31	16⅘	38–	54+	8
9:32—11:18	19¼	32⅔	54⅘	12½
11:19–26	16⅔	40	60	...
11:27—12:25	19½	28	69½	2½

CONCLUSIONS FROM THE TABLE

First, the general average varies *ca.* 100 per cent.—from less than 10 to 19½ per page.

Secondly, the percentage of ascriptives varies over 100 per cent.—from 28 per cent. to 63.

Thirdly, the percentage of adverbials varies less than 100 per cent.—from 37 to 69½ per cent.

Fourthly, the percentage of complementary participles varies from zero to 13½.

Fifthly, chap. 8 seems to be a line of cleavage between the earlier and later parts of Pe. The average is much smaller prior to chap. 8 and much larger from chap. 8 on. The ascriptives are more numerous and the adverbials less numerous prior to chap. 8 (except in secs. 6:1–7 and 11:27—12:25). 6:1–7 has the smallest percentage of ascriptives and the largest proportion of adverbials, while 11:27—12:25 has the next smallest percentage of ascriptives and the next largest proportion of adverbials. The early chapters contain rather more complementary participles, but chap. 8 following, fewer. Yet, there are two sections in chaps. 1–7 (both short) containing no complementary participles at all, while one very short section in chaps. 8–12 contains none.

Sixthly, such variety of participial usage would suggest a plurality of authors for Pe, were it not probable that variety in the literary character of the different sections and variety of usage in the possible written sources (for portions, at least) largely account for the variant participial usage in the different sections.

Sec. 90. The Participial Usage in the Subdivisions of Pa

These chapters naturally fall into the following sections: chaps. 13 and 14; 15:1–35; 15:36—18:22; 18:23—19:20; 19:21—21:14; 21:15—24:27; chaps. 25 and 26; 27:1—28:16; 28:17–31.

Chaps. 13 and 14 (Paul's first missionary journey) contain 105 participles, an average of 18½ per page, a little over 30 per cent. ascriptive, nearly 68 per cent. adverbial, not quite 2 per cent. complementary. These figures are near to those of Pa,[1] there being a few more ascriptives (probably due to the address in chap. 13 which contains two or three quotations from the Septuagint and which is somewhat Hebraistic in tone) and a few less adverbials.

15:1–35 (the Jerusalem conference) contains 37 participles, an average of 14¼ per page, ca. 27 per cent. ascriptive, 70¼ per cent. adverbial, and ca. 2¾ per cent. complementary. Two things are notable in these figures: an average lower than that of the preceding section and that of Pa, and the similarity of proportion between ascriptive, adverbial, and complementary participles as compared with the ratio of Pa. Hence, this section probably

[1] Pa has an average of 19 per page, ca. 24 per cent. ascriptive, 73½ per cent. adverbial, 2½ per cent. complementary.

comes from the same author, while his Jerusalem source may have helped to determine the lower average of this section.

15:36—18:22 (Paul's second missionary journey) has 144 participles, an average of $18\frac{3}{4}$ per page, $20\frac{1}{2}$ per cent. ascriptive, $77\frac{1}{4}$ per cent. adverbial, and 2+ per cent. complementary. That is, the ascriptive and complementary participles are used less frequently, but adverbials more copiously, which is, doubtless, due to the exclusively narrative nature of this section and its vivid description.

This section contains one of the "We" passages, 16:10–17, which averages 20 per page, 40 per cent. ascriptive, 60 per cent. adverbial. These figures might suggest that a different hand furnished the "We" passage, yet it is not impossible for the same hand to have varied, in participial usage, this much in so short a section (21 lines).

18:23—19:20 (early part of Paul's third missionary journey) has 40 participles, an average of $20\frac{1}{3}$ per page, 35 per cent. ascriptive, 65 per cent. adverbial. This section is very similar to the first "We" passage. There is a different ratio of ascriptives and adverbials as compared with that of Pa, yet not a greater difference than we find in the work of the same author.

19:21—21:14 (later part of Paul's third missionary journey) has 113 participles, $25\frac{2}{3}$ per cent. ascriptive, $72\frac{7}{12}$ per cent. adverbial, and $1\frac{3}{4}$ per cent. complementary. These figures are so near to those of Pa as to cast no doubt upon the unity of authorship. This section includes two "We" passages (lacking four verses of the second), but also two addresses, that of the Ephesian town clerk and that of Paul to the Ephesian elders. The narrative of the "We" passages and the argumentation of the addresses counteract each other and so preserve the uniformity of the whole section.

21:15—24:27 (Paul's arrest in Jerusalem and first trial in Caesarea) has 180 participles, an average of $20\frac{1}{3}$ per page, $27\frac{1}{4}$ per cent. ascriptive, $67\frac{3}{4}$ per cent. adverbial, and 5 per cent. complementary. These figures are too near to those of Pa to suggest plurality of authors.

Chaps. 25 and 26 (Paul's subsequent trials in Caesarea) contain 70 participles, an average of $15\frac{5}{9}$ per page, *ca.* 23 per cent. ascriptive, 74 per cent. adverbial, and *ca.* 3 per cent. complementary. Excepting the much smaller average, which is, doubtless, due to the addresses, the participial usage of this section is strikingly similar to that of Pa.

27:1—28:16 (voyage to Rome, including the shipwreck) has 102 participles, an average of $24\frac{1}{10}$ per page, $16\frac{2}{3}$ per cent. ascriptive, $80\frac{2}{3}$ per cent. adverbial, and $2\frac{4}{4}$ per cent. complementary. This, the longest "We" passage, is highly descriptive, being nearly all narrative; hence the small number of ascriptives and the large number of adverbials. Bearing this in mind, it is not impossible that the same hand that wrote Pa also wrote this section. At any rate, there is not so great a difference in participial usage here as we found in different sections of Pe and in different portions of Romans.

28:17–31 (Paul in Rome) contains 18 participles, an average of $13\frac{1}{2}$ per page, $16\frac{2}{3}$ per cent. ascriptive and $83\frac{1}{3}$ per cent. adverbial. The ratio between the ascriptive and the adverbial participles is almost the same as that in the last "We" passage. The low average for this section is due to the fact that 14 lines of it constitute an address and 10 lines of the address are quoted from the Septuagint. Yet, the large number of adverbials seems to indicate the free composition of the author.

SEC. 91.   TABLE ILLUSTRATING THE SUBDIVISIONS OF PA

Section	Average per Page of 30 Lines	Ascriptive Per cent.	Adverbial Per cent.	Complementary Per cent.
Chaps. 13 and 14.........	$18\frac{1}{2}$	$30+$	$68-$	$2-$
15:1–35	$14\frac{1}{4}$	27	$70\frac{1}{2}$	$2\frac{3}{4}$
15:36—18:22.............	$18\frac{3}{4}$	$20\frac{1}{2}$	$77\frac{1}{4}$	$2+$
18:23—19:20.............	$20\frac{3}{5}$	35	65	....
19:21—21:14.............	20	$25\frac{3}{4}$	$72\frac{7}{13}$	$1\frac{3}{4}$
21:15—24:27.............	$20\frac{1}{2}$	$27\frac{1}{4}$	$67\frac{1}{4}$	5
Chaps. 25 and 26.........	$15\frac{5}{8}$	23	74	ca. 3
27:1—28:16.............	$24\frac{1}{10}$	$16\frac{2}{3}$	$80\frac{2}{3}$	ca. 3
28:17–31................	$13\frac{1}{2}$	$16\frac{2}{3}$	$83\frac{1}{3}$	....

SOME OBSERVATIONS ON THESE FIGURES

First, the average is fairly regular throughout Pa, except in section 15:1–35, where the average is small because of the addresses, the quotation and Septuagint tone, and in chaps. 25 and 26 in which occur Pauline addresses and a Septuagint tone, which facts help to explain an average below that of Pa.

Secondly, the percentage of ascriptives varies over 100 per cent. in the different sections (as in Pe), from $16\frac{2}{3}$ to 35 per cent.

Thirdly, the percentage of adverbials varies about 25 per cent., from 65 to $83\frac{1}{3}$ per cent.

Fourthly, the percentage of complementary participles varies from zero to 5 per cent.

Fifthly, the variations in Pa are much less than in Pe, the percentage of variation being equal nowhere except in ascriptives.

Sixthly, after taking account of the variations due to literary form and to the sources in different sections, we may say that there is a striking uniformity in participial usage throughout Pa.

CHAPTER XII

THE SOURCES OF THE BOOK OF ACTS SEEN IN THE LIGHT OF PARTICIPIAL USAGE

SEC. 92. INTRODUCTORY STATEMENT

If the unity of authorship is accepted, the extreme variations in participial usage (as in other phases of style) can be explained satisfactorily only on the hypothesis of written sources whose literary peculiarities influenced the author.

We have established, beyond a reasonable doubt, in Part I (see various summary tables) that the participial usage of the Septuagint (which is to some extent Hebraistic) is quite different from the style of the classical or κοινή Greek. There is so great a difference (especially in the number of participles and the ratio between ascriptives and adverbials) that one is fairly safe in concluding, from the participial usage, the Hellenic or Hebraistic character of a certain piece of Greek. That is, if the number is very small and the ascriptives overwhelmingly predominate over the adverbials, it is probable that the piece of Greek is not pure literary κοινή, but Hebraistic or vernacular Greek (according to facts on p. 10). And although it is sometimes difficult to discriminate between the Hebraistic and vernacular Greek style, yet it is easy to discriminate between the style of the literary κοινή and the Hebraistic Greek. As seen above the style of Pa is rather Hellenic, while that of Pe is more Hebraistic in tone.

On the other hand, if we accept a plurality of authors (or editors, or redactors, who in any considerable degree "worked over" the material) it is difficult to conclude from variations in participial usage in different sections that different sources must lie at the basis of these different sections.

The facts set forth in the last chapter seem to point to the unity of the book. Then let us examine the different portions on the assumption that the book is practically a literary unit, and see what light the participial usage throws on possible written sources.

SEC. 93. SPITTA'S HYPOTHESIS TESTED BY PARTICIPIAL USAGE

Spitta accepts (see p. 49 above) two sources running parallel from the beginning to the end of the book, that now a paragraph (or longer section, or even verse, or line) is taken from A (the work of Luke and constituting about two-thirds of the book) and now a paragraph (or longer or shorter section) is taken from B (a Jewish-Christian source). The redactor also adds a few lines occasionally.

Let us examine some sections from 6:1 ff., and see if the participial usage justifies Spitta's hypothesis.

6:1–6, 9–12a he regards as from A; 6:7, 8, 12b–15 from B. 6:1–6 contains 5 participles, 20 per cent. ascriptive and 80 per cent. adverbial. 6:7, 8 has no participles at all. 6:9–12a contains 4 participles, 75 per cent. ascriptive and 25 per cent. complementary (though συνζητοῦντες might be considered adverbial instead of ascriptive). 6:12b–15 contains 6 participles, 33⅓ per cent. each ascriptive, adverbial, and complementary.

Now the first section, vss. 1–6, agrees in participial usage fairly well with the "We" source, as Spitta has supposed. It must be conceded that vss. 7 and 8, since they contain no participial clause but do contain καὶ . . . . τε, and δέ five times for uniting the clauses of these two verses, are Hebraistic in tone. But the objector might say, There is not a participle in vss. 4 and 5 in the supposed "We" section, vss. 1–6, and surely the participle might have been easily used at the beginning of vs. 5. So the participial usage of 6:1–6, 7, 8, while not condemning Spitta's hypothesis, does not necessarily confirm it.

In 6:9–12a (A) the participial usage is decidedly against Spitta's hypothesis, even if συνζητοῦντες be construed as adverbial (if it is regarded as ascriptive the style is overwhelmingly against his hypothesis). The participial usage of 6:12b–15 does not speak clearly for or against his hypothesis.

7:2–54, 57, 58a are from A, while 7:55, 56, 58b, 59–61 are from B. In the A-section occur 38 participles, 31 per cent. ascriptive, ca. 64 per cent. adverbial, and ca. 5 per cent. complementary. In the B-section occur 10 participles, only 10 per cent. ascriptive, 60 per cent. adverbial and 30 per cent. complementary. According to Spitta this section is more Hebraistic than "Lukan," but the participial usage shows just the opposite. Hence the participial usage shows Spitta's division of the last verses of chap. 7 to be arbitrary.

Spitta puts all of chap. 8 in B, except 1b, and 2 (A), and vss. 4 and 40b which are by the redactor. In 1b and 2 there is not a participle. In 1a, 3, 5–40a are found 42 participles, 38 per cent. ascriptive, 57⅓ per cent. adverbial, and less than 5 per cent. complementary. This can scarcely be classed as Hebraistic. Moreover, in the section which Spitta regards as "Lukan" (A) there is not a single participle. This is strange. The facts of participial usage in chap. 8 are clearly against Spitta.

Chap. 9 he regards as from B, except vss. 4 and 5, which are from the redactor. In the A-section occur 59 participles, 33⅔ per cent. ascriptive, 62¾ per cent. adverbial, ca. 3⅓ per cent. complementary. This is surely more "Lukan" than Hebraistic in participial usage. Moreover, the average for this chapter (21 per page) is decidedly against its composition by a Jewish writer (unless the style of the source is completely ignored by the later hand).

Chap. 10 he regards as from B, except vss. 36–43 by the redactor. The B-portion contains 50 participles, 36 per cent. ascriptive, 50 per cent. adverbial, and 14 per cent. complementary. In vss. 36–43 occur 11 participles, 54½ per cent. ascriptive and 45½ per cent. adverbial. That is, the portion ascribed by Spitta to the redactor is more Hebraistic than the section which he says comes directly from the Jewish source.

Chap. 11 is from B, except vss. 19–21 and 27–30 (from A) and 22, 24b–26 (from the redactor). The B-portion contains 20 participles, 30 per cent. ascriptive, 50 per cent. adverbial, and 20 per cent. complementary. The A-section contains 10 participles, 50 per cent. each ascriptive and adverbial. The figures for both sections are against Spitta's hypothesis, for the section which should be more Hebraistic is more "Lukan" and vice versa.

Chap. 12 is from B, except vs. 25 (A). Vss. 1–24 contain 36 participles, 25 per cent. ascriptive, 72 per cent. adverbial, less than 3 per cent. complementary, while vs. 25 has three participles, 33⅓ per cent. ascriptive, the rest adverbial. That is, the B-portion, according to Spitta, is more "Lukan" than the "Lukan" verse itself (25).

According to Spitta, the most of chaps. 13–28 comes from A, but some short sections (very few longer ones) come from B. Let us examine the participial tone of these B-sections in chaps. 13–28.

In chaps. 13 and 14 Spitta regards 13:6–12, 44–49, 52; 14:3, 8–15a, 18–20 as coming from B. This B-portion contains 40 participles, 25 per cent. ascriptive, 70 per cent. adverbial, and ca. 5 per cent. complementary. These are strange figures for a Jewish-written source (unless radically changed by a later hand). According to Sec. 90, chaps. 13 and 14 have 30 per cent. ascriptive, 68 per cent. adverbial, and ca. 2 per cent. complementary. Hence, it appears that Spitta's Jewish source in these chapters is less Jewish and more Lukan than the chapters as a whole.

Chap. 15 is divided into vss. 35–41 (from A) and vss. 1–4, 13–33 (from B), the rest from the redactor. The A-section has 9 participles, one-third ascriptive and two-thirds adverbial (with the possibility that one counted ascriptive may be adverbial). The B-section contains 28 participles, 32¼ per cent. ascriptive and 67⅔ adverbial. The participial usage is so similar in A and B as not to suggest a plurality of sources.

[In chap. 16 he regards vss. 22–34, 36b as from B, in which occur 18 participles (three-fourths of page), 88⅔ per cent. adverbial and 11⅛ complementary with not one ascriptive. These figures, showing a piece of Greek so un-Hebraistic, are decidedly against Spitta.

Only two other long sections in chaps. 13–28 are regarded by Spitta as from B, 19:10*b*–20, 24–40, and 23.:1–10. The former section contains 43 participles, 39¾ per cent. ascriptive, *ca.* 58 per cent. adverbial, and 2⅓ per cent. complementary. This section is a little more Hebraistic in participial usage than other sections ascribed by Spitta to B, but the Hebraistic tone is too slight to reflect a purely Jewish written source, since so large a percentage of adverbial participles is found in no Jewish writer of the New Testament, except Mark (whose participial usage is probably due to his intimate intercourse with non-Jewish people in his later life and to the marked narrative style of his gospel).

In 23:1–10 are found 14 participles, 42⅔ per cent. ascriptive and 57¼ per cent. adverbial, and hence the section does not strongly reflect a Jewish-written source.

Upon the whole it may be said that the participial usage of chaps. 6–12 does not entirely condemn Spitta's hypothesis, nor does it confirm it. The same may be said of chaps. 13–28, though his hypothesis that the most of these chapters comes from the Lukan, or "We," source is strongly substantiated by the participial usage.

Since J. Weiss holds virtually the same hypothesis as Spitta (except he thinks that chaps. 1–5 come from one source and the address of Stephen is a unit); since also Jüngst (1895) simply modified Spitta's hypothesis (differing as to the extent of the sources and regarding source B as Ebionitic and identical to a source of the Third Gospel), we do not consider their hypotheses in detail. But the participial usage seems to suggest too much literary unity in Acts (which J. Weiss concedes) to admit of its being pieced together by a redactor from such dissimilar (and often meager) fragments.

SEC. 94. FEINE'S HYPOTHESIS IN THE LIGHT OF PARTICIPIAL USAGE

In 1891, Feine put forth the hypothesis that most of 1:1—11:24 comes from a pre-canonical document of the Third Gospel, parts of chaps. 7–9 and 11 coming from another source (the basis of chaps. 13–28).

He regards as coming from this latter source 6:1–6, participles 20 per cent. ascriptive and 80 per cent. adverbial; 6:12–14, participles 25 per cent. each ascriptive and adverbial, 50 per cent. complementary; 7:2–21, participles 10 per cent. each ascriptive and complementary, 80 per cent. adverbial; 7:29–34, participles, all adverbial, but small average, 11 per page; 7:44–50, 50 per cent. each ascriptive and adverbial; 7:57, 58, one-third ascriptive, two-thirds adverbial; 8:25–40 (about which Feine hesitates), 23½ per cent. ascriptive, 70½ per cent. adverbial, 6 per cent. complementary; 9:1–30, nearly 39 per cent. ascriptive, 53¾ per cent. adverbial, *ca.* 8 per cent. complementary; 11:25–30, 40 per cent. ascriptive and 60 per cent. adverbial.

These sections (except 9:1–30) it must be conceded, according to parti-cipial usage, are more similar in style to chaps. 13–28 than to the most of chaps. 1–12, excepting the smaller average. Hence, while the parti-cipial usage in chaps. 1–12 is not directly against Feine's hypothesis, it is surely not strongly in favor of it.

Sec. 95. Carl Clemen's Hypothesis in the Light of Participial Usage

In 1893 (*Die Chronologie*), again in 1895 (SK), Carl Clemen published what is perhaps the most elaborate hypothesis as to the sources in the Book of Acts. He regards the Book of Acts as the literary product of two redactors, one friendly (Rj), the other hostile, to the Jewish-Christian point of view (Ra), based on two sources, HPe (*History of Peter*) and HPa (*History of Paul*). He regards the two sources as not simply chronicles in their respective spheres of early Christian activity, but as having passed through a literary history of their own before being used by the two redac-tors in producing the Book of Acts. Of course, he regards the most of chaps. 1–12 as from HPe and the most of chaps. 13–28 as from HPa. But he supposes that one or the other of the redactors inserted many short or long passages in both parts of the book.

We have seen above that the participial usage favors and even demands the general division of the book into two portions. But how does it bear on Clemen's hypothesis of a redaction of these by two hostile hands?

He regards as the work of Ra in chaps. 1–12, 4:36—5:11, participles, 37 per cent. ascriptive and 63 per cent. adverbial, average, 20; 8:14–25, average, 14, 20 per cent. ascriptive, 70 per cent. adverbial, 10 per cent. complementary; 9:1–31, average, 16⅘ (over 17 if ἀναστάς, vs. 11, be included), nearly 38 per cent. ascriptive, a little over 54 per cent. adverbial, *ca.* 8 per cent. complementary; 11:27–30, average, 15, 50 per cent. each ascriptive and adverbial; 12:1–25, average, *ca.* 22, 28 per cent. ascriptive, 69⅔ per cent. adverbial, 2⅓ per cent. complementary.

These sections in chaps. 1–12 do have a much larger average than the rest of these chapters, which shows them to be at least un-Jewish in tone, if not anti-Jewish (as Clemen claims). The ratio between the ascriptive, adverbial, and complementary participles indicates an un-Jewish source or composition, or both, for these sections.

In chaps. 13–28 Clemen regards as the work of Ra, 13:44–50, average, 15, 50 per cent. each ascriptive and adverbial; 15:5–12, 19, 23–33, average, 15¾, 19 per cent. ascriptive, 76 per cent. adverbial, *ca.* 5 per cent. complementary; 18:6, average, *ca.* 30, all adverbial; 20:25–35, 38*a*, average, 15, 41⅔ per cent. ascriptive, 50 per cent. adverbial, 8⅓ per cent. complementary; 28:25–28, average, 8 (due probably to a long quotation with only one participle), all adverbial.

These sections average only *ca.* 15 (except 18:6 which is too short to reckon on), which is about the average of the Jewish portion of the Book of Acts. Also the ratio between ascriptives and adverbials agrees more nearly with that of chaps. 1–12 than with that of chaps. 13–28. Therefore, the participial usage in these sections is *against* Clemen's hypothesis that an anti-Jewish redactor added them.

Let us now look at some Rj sections (limiting ourselves to those in chaps. 13–28, since there are very few in chaps. 1–12).

15:1–4, participles all adverbial, average 11½; 15:13–18, average, 10 (but most of this section is quoted), 75 per cent. ascriptive and 25 per cent. adverbial; 15:20–22, average, 17½, 60 per cent. ascriptive and 40 per cent. adverbial; 16:1–3, average, 9, 50 per cent. each ascriptive and adverbial; 21:20*b*–26, average, 18, 36$\frac{4}{11}$ per cent. ascriptive, 63$\frac{7}{11}$ adverbial; 22:1–16, 19–21, average, 22, 55 per cent. ascriptive, 41¾ adverbial, and 3¼ complementary; 23:1–10, average, 16¼, 39 per cent. ascriptive, 61 per cent. adverbial; 28:16–24, average, 15, 25 per cent. ascriptive, 75 per cent adverbial.

Excepting 15:1–4 and 28:16–24, the participial usage in these sections as to the ratio between ascriptives and adverbials is like that of chaps. 1–12 rather than that of chaps. 13–28. The average varies, about half resembling that of the first portion, the other half, that of the second portion. These figures then only slightly confirm Clemen's hypothesis.

To conclude as to Clemen's hypothesis, his general supposition of two basal histories (HPe and HPa) fairly harmonizes with the participial usage of the book, but his supposition of an anti-Jewish writer who works over many passages is contrary to the participial usage and his supposition of a Jewish hand in certain sections is only partially confirmed by the participial usage. Hence we ask, as to the last sections (Rj), since they are intensely Jewish and since they contain two of the Pauline addresses (which are Jewish in participial style), could not the Jewish tone in participial usage, as well as in other stylistic features too, be more naturally accounted for by supposing a Jewish-Christian source which influenced the style of the author?

SEC. 96. THE SOURCE HYPOTHESIS IN HARMONY WITH THE
PARTICIPIAL USAGE

Wendt hesitates to state with precision the limits of the various sources in the Book of Acts.   He thinks that the "We" source is the only distinctly written source, not only for chaps. 13–28 (most), but that it is the basis of many sections in chaps. 1–12 (11:19 f.; 8:1, 4; chaps. 6 and 7, and possibly some passages in chaps. 1–5, though he regards the most of chaps. 1–5 based on well-defined traditions). The participial usage does not confirm Wendt's hypothesis of no written sources except the "We" document. It is difficult to see how the style should be so different in the early chapters from that of the later portion of the book, if one writer, and that a non-Jewish writer (as Wendt holds), composed the whole book, unless he had before him Jewish-Christian written sources for these early chapters.

On the other hand, Hilgenfeld holds to three written sources: A, the Acts of Peter, 1:15—5:42; 10:1—11:18; B, the Acts of the Seven, most of chaps. 6–8; C, the Acts of Paul, the most of chaps. 13–28 and small portions of chaps. 7, 8, 9, and 11.

Let us look at the facts of the participial usage in detail in the various sections of the book.

1:1–14 (WH's first paragraph) averages 16½, with 36¾ per cent. ascriptive, 58 per cent. adverbial, and 5¼ per cent. complementary.   This is a mixture of Jewish Greek (similar to that in Luke 1:5—2:52) and literary κοινή Greek (like that of the late chapters of Acts).   But suppose we make the paragraph between vss. 11 and 12, we find that 1:1–11 has an average of 18 per page, 20 per cent. ascriptive, 73½ per cent. adverbial, and 6⅔ per cent. complementary, a piece of Greek closely resembling the free composition of the late chapters of the Book of Acts.   This is the logical paragraph division, since vss. 1–11 describe Jesus' last interview with the disciples and his ascension, while vs. 12 begins a line of thought connected with the return to and stay in Jerusalem.

1:12—5:16 constitutes a section fairly uniform in participial usage, averaging 12½ per page, with 45½ per cent. ascriptive, 51¼ per cent. adverbial, and 3¼ per cent. complementary.   These figures are very close to those of Mark's gospel (only Mark is a little less Jewish in participial usage).   Hence, we must conclude that, if a non-Jewish writer composed this section (1:12—5:16) as it now stands, he had before him a Jewish-Christian document and followed it closely.

5:17-33 (story of Peter and John's miraculous deliverance) has an average of nearly 20 per page, 24 per cent. ascriptive, 66⅔ per cent. adverbial, and *ca.* 9⅓ per cent. complementary, which figures betray the style of the non-Jewish κοινή writer of the last chapters of the Book of Acts. This probably suggests that this story was not put in writing (being so remarkable it was easy to remember) and that the author freely composed this.

5:34-42 (most of it Gamaliel's address) betrays a Hebraistic style in its average of 9½ participles per page, while the absence of ascriptives and 71⅔ per cent. adverbials show the free composition of the non-Jewish writer.

10:1—11:18 (Cornelius episode, the next most Jewish piece of Greek in chaps. 1-12) averages 17½ with 37½ per cent. ascriptive, 48¾ per cent. adverbial, and 13¾ per cent. complementary. This section is much less Jewish, as is shown by the ratio between the ascriptives and adverbials, and by the large average. It is not improbable that the basis of this Cornelius section was a document written by Mark, the reputed interpreter of Peter, and that this source was freely worked over by the author of the book. Or, this section, judged from its participial usage, may not have a written source at all, but may have been freely composed by the author from a tradition (and if Luke be the author he may have heard Mark tell it in Rome, both being there with Paul, according to Col. 4:10, 14).

Chaps. 6-8 (Stephen and Philip sections) betray a uniformity of participial usage, averaging 12⅘ per page with 35 per cent. ascriptive, *ca.* 56 per cent. adverbial, and 9 per cent. complementary. By comparison with 10:1—11:18, we see that these chapters are less Hebraistic when we consider the ratio of ascriptive, adverbial, and complementary participles, but are more Hebraistic when we consider the average. Yet, the average is doubtless diminished in these chapters by two causes, the presence of so much Septuagint matter and a long address in chap. 7. By comparison with 1:12—5:16, we see that chaps. 6-8 are less Hebraistic in participial usage. So this whole section seems to be less Jewish than the Jewish-Christian sections, 1:12—5:16, 34-42, and 10:1—11:18. Is the difference in style great enough to suggest a different source, that is, a Hellenistic-Christian source as distinguished from the Jewish-Christian source? Or, is the difference in participial usage due to the working-over by the author and to the different literary point of view in the sections? On the other hand, it must be observed that the style is so different in chaps. 6-8 from that of the late chapters of the book that it is scarcely conceivable that these chapters should have been composed without written sources as a basis.

Chap. 12 averages over 22 per page with 28 per cent. ascriptive, $69\frac{2}{3}$ per cent. adverbial, and $2\frac{1}{3}$ per cent. complementary. The source must be Jewish, since it deals with the Jerusalem church, but it could not well be a Jewish-Christian written source, judged from the participial usage, unless it be supposed that the author completely changed the participial usage of the source. It seems best to regard chap. 12 (like 5:17–33) as the free composition of the non-Jewish author, based on a Jewish-Christian tradition.

9:1–31 (conversion and early Christian activity of Saul) has an average of $16\frac{4}{5}$, nearly 38 per cent. ascriptive, over 54 per cent. adverbial, and *ca.* 8 per cent. complementary. This section is not to be divided between vss. 19 and 20, since the participial usage is similar throughout the section (except all the complementary participles occur in vss. 1–19, but this is due to the vision described). This section is not so strongly Hellenic as the late chapters in the Book of Acts, nor is it Hebraistic. Did it come from a Jewish or a non-Jewish source? It seems unlikely, judged from the participial usage, that this section comes from the "We" source, since the average and ratio between ascriptives and adverbials differ so much from those in the "We" source. The participial usage suggests a Jewish source which has been worked over by a non-Jewish writer, but it is not probable that the section comes from a Jewish-Christian written source. The most probable solution, suggested by the participial usage, is that this section is based on a well-defined tradition, first told by Paul himself (this helping to account for the Hebraistic tone in its participial usage), handed down by his friends in its Jewish dress, but worked over by the non-Jewish author who gives it its Hellenic tone. The fact that there are in this account of Saul's conversion details differing from those in the accounts in chaps. 22 and 26, and the lack of details in his early work in Damascus and Jerusalem (vss. 20–31 containing a bare outline) confirm the hypothesis of an unwritten source for 9:1–31.

9:32–43 (a Petrine missionary tour) has an average of 25 per page, 22 per cent. ascriptive and 78 per cent. adverbial. These figures are strongly against a Jewish-Christian written source. It is likely from a Jewish-Christian tradition and freely composed by the non-Jewish author.

11:19–30 (the gospel in Antioch) averages *ca.* 16 participles per page with $42\frac{6}{7}$ per cent. ascriptive and $57\frac{1}{7}$ per cent. adverbial. This section did not then likely come from the "We" source. Its participial usage agrees more nearly with that of the Hellenistic-Christian source (chaps. 6–8), and vs. 19, which speaks of "those who were scattered by the tribulation that arose over Stephen," suggests a Hellenistic-Christian source.

In chaps. 13–28 the main source is doubtless the "We" document, since it is so vivid and vigorous in style. Nor is the "We" document to be limited to the four passages (16:1–10; 20:5–16; 21:1–18; 27:1—28:16) in which the pronoun "we" or "us" occurs, because the participial usage within and just without the "We" passages is remarkably similar (see pp. 17 and 18). Of course, where addresses occur in the context of the "We" passages their presence diminishes the average and the percentage of adverbials.

The following sections in chaps. 13–28 are probably not from the "We" document:

15:1–35 (Jerusalem conference) has an average of $14\frac{1}{4}$, but the adverbial percentage of $70\frac{1}{4}$ shows that it was thoroughly worked over by the non-Jewish author.

16:1–5 (circumcision of Timothy and delivery of the decrees) averages only $7\frac{1}{2}$ per page with two-thirds ascriptive and one-third adverbial (no marks of the "We" document, but intensely Jewish).

Possibly 19:1–20 (Pauline miracles in Ephesus) is not from the "We" document. It contains 60 per cent. ascriptive and 40 per cent. adverbial, with an average of $18\frac{3}{4}$ per page, which facts probably show that it is from a Hellenistic-Christian source but freely worked over by the author.

21:20*b*–26 (Paul's vow at James's suggestion) has 40 per cent. ascriptive and 60 per cent. adverbial, with an average of 17 per page. Hence the section is probably from a Jewish-Christian source freely worked over.

22:1–21, with an average of $24\frac{2}{7}$, but 50 per cent. ascriptive, and only 41 per cent. adverbial, is doubtful as to source. It may be a part of the "We" document, but the participial usage is against the supposition. It is more probable, according to participial usage, that it is from a tradition told first by Paul in Aramaic and then freely worked over by the author of the book.

23:1–10, with an average of *ca.* 18, but $42\frac{6}{7}$ per cent. ascriptive, $57\frac{1}{7}$ per cent. adverbial, has a somewhat Hebraistic tone, but seems to be a free composition by a non-Jewish writer.

Chaps. 25 and 26 (see p. 55) have a low average, $15\frac{5}{8}$, but probably the presence of addresses and the absence of pure narrative throughout account for this. But the ratio between ascriptives and adverbials is similar to that of the "We" document from which they probably are taken.

The account of Paul's conversion in 26:9–18, according to participial usage, seems to be nearer to the story as (probably) told by Paul than either 9:1–19 or 22:4–16, the average being only $14\frac{1}{3}$. Yet, there is a great change in the account as worked over by the author, which is shown by the large percentage of adverbials (see p. 20 for facts). The participial usage does not at all make it clear that the accounts of Paul's conversion in chaps. 22 and 26 belong to the "We" document. It seems to suggest the Pauline manner of telling the story modified by the author.

28:17–31, though having a smaller average, which is largely due to the Septuagint quotation, is strikingly similar in participial usage to the "We" document. This section may be based on it, or on tradition.

RECAPITULATION OF THE SOURCE HYPOTHESIS IN HARMONY WITH THE PARTICIPIAL USAGE

First, the Jewish-Christian written source includes 1:12—5:18, 34–42; 10:1—11:18; 15:1–35; 16:1–5 (?); 21:20*b*–26.

Secondly, the Hellenistic-Christian written source, chaps. 6–8; 11:19–30 (?); 19:11–20 (?).

Thirdly, the "We" document, chaps. 13 and 14; 15:36–41; 16:6—21:20*a* (perhaps, excepting 19:11–20); 21:27—26:32 (perhaps, excepting 22:1–21; 23:1–10 [?]; 26:9–18) and 27:1—28:16.

Fourthly, unwritten source, Jewish-Christian tradition, 1:1–11; 5:17–33; 9:1–31, 32–43; 19:11–20 (?); 22:1–21; 26:9–18; 28:17–31 (possibly 23:1–10).

CHAPTER XIII

THE AUTHORSHIP OF THE BOOK OF ACTS IN THE LIGHT OF THE PARTICIPIAL USAGE

SEC. 97. PRELIMINARY STATEMENT

The New Testament scholarship of the world has been for nearly half a century, and is now, divided on the Lukan authorship of the Book of Acts. For the Lukan authorship stand Credner, B. Weiss, Klostermann, Renan, Hobart, Ramsay, Hawkins (Sir John), Plummer, Vogel, Blass, Harnack, Zahn, Ropes, Burkitt (F. C.), etc.

On the other hand, against the Lukan authorship stand Königsmann, De Wette, Baur, Zeller, Hilgenfeld, Holtzmann (H. J.), Overbeck, Hausrath, Weizsäcker, Wendt, Schürer, Pfleiderer, von Soden, Spitta, Jülicher, J. Weiss, Knopf, C. Clemen, McGiffert, etc. Sorof thinks Timothy is the author.

Now let us see what light is thrown upon this problem by the participial usage.

SEC. 98. IS THE AUTHOR OF THE THIRD GOSPEL THE AUTHOR OF THE BOOK OF ACTS ?

From the facts stated on pp. 19, 20, and 23, we make the following observations:

First, the average in the Third Gospel is nearer to that of the first portion of the Book of Acts than to that of the whole book.

Secondly, the ratio between the three great classes of participles in the Third Gospel is much nearer to that of the first portion than to that of the whole book (however, the only very significant difference is the different percentage of adverbial and complementary participles).

Thirdly, the average in the Third Gospel is much smaller than in the second portion of the Book of Acts.

Fourthly, the ratio between ascriptive, adverbial, and complementary participles in the Third Gospel differs considerably from that in the second portion of the Book of Acts.

Fifthly, the average and the ratio of ascriptives and adverbials in the Third Gospel differ slightly from the average and ratio of ascriptives and adverbials in the whole Book of Acts.

From these observations we see how easily eminent scholars differ as to the style and authorship of the Book of Acts. It remains for us to weigh the probabilities growing out of the above differences and agreements.

Must the author of the Book of Acts and of the Third Gospel be the same writer, according to participial usage (the conclusion reached by Harnack on the basis of general style and diction) ?   Or must we predicate different authors for the two books because of the different participial usage observed above ?

There are three facts to be held in mind in answering these questions:

First, the Third Gospel is more dependent on Jewish-Christian (doubtless written) sources than is the Book of Acts.   It is true that much of Acts, chaps. 1–12, seems to be based on Jewish-Christian sources and so is influenced by the Hebraistic style characteristic of such sources.   But the proportion of material in the Book of Acts coming from Jewish-Christian written sources is much smaller than in the Third Gospel.

Secondly, the Book of Acts is more strictly narrative than the Third Gospel, which fact naturally affects the style of the same author (tested by us in classical authors, as well as in Acts).   Though there are many addresses reported in the Book of Acts, the most of them are short, and the great mass of the book is narrative of tours and movements of missionary work.

Thirdly, the author in the Third Gospel seems to reproduce his sources more rigidly than the author in the Book of Acts.   This is specially true in chaps. 1 and 2 (except preface), but even in the rest of the book the author is influenced (apparently) by the Hebraistic tone of his sources. The preface is good Greek.   This proves that the author could, when untrammeled by his sources, write good Greek, and it also proves (probably) that in the rest of the book where the Greek is less pure the author is more or less influenced by the style of his sources.

Then what bearing have these three propositions, combined with the above observations, on the authorship of the Third Gospel and the Book of Acts ?   The more rigid adherence to Jewish-Christian sources in the Third Gospel and the presence of more narrative in the Book of Acts would help to explain the differences observed above.   That is, the differences of participial usage in the two books can easily be explained by the nature of the sources, the apparent method of the author in dealing with these sources in the two books, and by the literary character of the productions.   Hence the differences of participial usage between the two books are not evidence against the unity of authorship for the two books. On the contrary, the similarity between the participial usage of the two books is so great, notwithstanding different kinds of sources in the two, as to point unmistakably to one author for the two books.

SEC. 99. IS THE AUTHOR OF THE "WE" PASSAGES THE AUTHOR OF THE BOOK OF ACTS?

The scholars who deny the Lukan authorship (see Sec. 97), as a rule, answer in the negative. What light does the participial usage throw upon this question? On the following page we submit a table giving the facts for the "We" passages and their immediate contexts, precedent and subsequent; also giving the facts for eleven sections in Luke, chaps. 10–19 (record of Perean ministry), of corresponding lengths and relations as to position.

SEC. 100. OBSERVATIONS ON TABLE ON PAGE 71

First, there is a marked similarity in average between the "We" passages and their immediate contexts, precedent and subsequent (except the 27 lines following 20:16 which include the address of James and the elders in Jerusalem to Paul, which fact doubtless accounts for the small average). Of course, the average of the "We" passages (23) is somewhat greater than that of the contexts, but the fact that they are pure narrative may account for this.

Secondly, the averages in the eleven sections of corresponding length in the Third Gospel show greater variations (from $7\frac{1}{3}$ to $18\frac{3}{4}$ per page, though all concede these sections in the Perean ministry to be the composition of one author based on one source [largely]) than do the "We" passages and their contexts (from $11\frac{1}{8}$ to $25\frac{1}{2}$).

Thirdly, the percentage of ascriptives in the "We" passages and their contexts varies from 8 per cent. to $41\frac{2}{3}$ (over 5 to 1), but the percentage of ascriptives in the corresponding sections of the Third Gospel varies from $11\frac{1}{4}$ to $71\frac{2}{7}$ (over 6 to 1).

Fourthly, the percentage of adverbials in the "We" passages and their contexts varies from $54\frac{6}{11}$ to 92 (ca. 70 per cent. of variation) while in the sections tested in Luke, chaps. 10–19, the variation ranges from 41 to $88\frac{8}{9}$ per cent. (over 100 per cent.).

Fifthly, the percentage of complementary participles in the "We" passages and their contexts varies from zero to $7\frac{3}{4}$, while that in the sections of the Third Gospel varies from zero to $14\frac{2}{7}$.

Sixthly, hence there is greater similarity of participial usage between the "We" passages and their contexts than we find in sections of corresponding length in Luke, chaps. 10–19.

Seventhly, if we consider the similarity between the average and ratio of ascriptives and adverbials in the "We" passages and their contexts as compared with those of the first portion, we notice that this similarity is

TABLE ILLUSTRATING THE PARTICIPIAL USAGE OF THE "WE" PASSAGES, THEIR CONTEXTS; AND ELEVEN SECTIONS OF CORRESPONDING LENGTH IN LUKE, CHAPS. 10–19

"We" Passages	Average	Ascriptive %	Adverbial %	Complementary %	Luke, chaps. 10–19, in Eleven Sections	Average	Ascriptive %	Adverbial %	Complementary %
16:10–17	20	40	60	....	10:1 f., 21 lines	7¾	40	60	....
21 lines preceding	18	41¼	58⅓	....	21 lines preceding	13	11½	88½	....
21 lines following	19	8	92	....	21 lines following	10	71³⁄₇	14²⁄₇	14²⁄₇
20:5–16	25½	30¾	69¼	....	14:1 f., 27 lines	18⅔	59	41	....
27 lines preceding	20	11	84	5	27 lines preceding	13¼	50	41⅔	8⅓
27 lines following	11½	40	60	....	27 lines following	11	50	50	....
21:1–18	23¼	16⅔	83⅓	....	15:1 f., 40 lines	18¾	24	76	....
40 lines preceding	16½	40¼	54¾	ca. 4¼	40 lines preceding	15¼	38	62	....
40 lines following	16½	29¼	66¾	4⅛	40 lines following	10¼	42¾	57¼	....
27:1–28:16	24¹⁄₁₀	16⅔	80¾	2¼	18:1 f., 127 lines	15⅚	39¾	59	1¼
127 lines preceding	15⅗	23⅛	73⅛	3⅛	127 lines preceding	9	36¼	60¼	2¾
Pauline portion	19	24	73¾	ca. 2¼	Book of Third Gospel	16⅔	40³⁄₁₀	55¼	4⅓
Petrine portion	15½	34⅓	57⅞	ca. 7¾					
Book of Acts	ca. 17¾	28¼	68	ca. 4					

remarkable, except in the few sections influenced by the Jewish-Christian sources, or by the literary character of the section (that is, whether it is address, narrative, etc.).

Eighthly, we observe furthermore that the dissimilarity between the "We" passages and their contexts as compared with the whole Book of Acts is not much greater than the dissimilarity between the eleven sections in the Third Gospel as compared with the whole Third Gospel. There is a somewhat greater difference in the ratio between ascriptives and adverbials and in the average in the Book of Acts, but this is probably due to the Jewish- and Hellenistic-Christian written sources which play a conspicuous part in chaps. 1–12.

Ninthly, conclusion: From these facts it is not to be asserted dogmatically that the participial usage of the Book of Acts proves that the author of the "We" passages is also the author of the book, and yet the participial usage is not at all in favor of different authors for the book and the "We" sections. So the participial usage seems to substantiate, in a collateral way, the conclusion that the original author of the "We" sections is also the final author of the Book of Acts.

SEC. 101. IS THE AUTHOR OF THE BOOK OF ACTS THE COMPANION OF PAUL CALLED LUKE THE PHYSICIAN?

On this question the participle has no direct answer. The theology of Paul may have influenced Luke's thinking and the matter of his books, but it is quite sure, from participial usage, that Paul's manner of writing did not impress itself on him. See on p. 23 how far different is the participial usage of Paul, of the Third Gospel, and of the Book of Acts.

If Luke the physician and missionary companion of Paul be the author of the Third Gospel, then it is very likely, from the participial usage, that he is the author of the "We" sections and of the Book of Acts.

CHAPTER XIV

COMPOSITION OF THE ADDRESSES IN THE BOOK OF ACTS IN THE LIGHT OF PARTICIPIAL USAGE

SEC. 102. PRELIMINARY STATEMENT

There are many addresses in the Book of Acts presented (apparently) as if composed originally by Peter, Gamaliel, Stephen, James, Paul, Felix, Festus, etc. Is the participial usage of these addresses different from that of the rest of the book, or is there a striking similarity which suggests the free composition of these addresses by the author of the book? In the Pauline addresses does the style resemble the style of Paul's letters closely enough to lead us to conclude that Paul himself composed these addresses and the author of the Book of Acts simply reproduced them in his book, or is the style so similar to that of the rest of the book as to compel us to conclude that the author of the book freely composed the addresses (of course, using Pauline material as the basis)?

For the facts of participial usage in the addresses see pp. 19 and 20.

SEC. 102. COMPOSITION OF THE PETRINE ADDRESSES

From the facts on p. 19 we make the following observations:

First, the average in them is $11\frac{4}{5}+$.

Secondly, the lowest average, 6 (except that in the short address to Simon Magus which is too short to use in an argument), is in the address to the Jerusalem Conference, and the highest average is in the address to Cornelius' household ($17\frac{8}{11}$).

Thirdly, the average of ascriptives in all his addresses is $48\frac{1}{3}$ per cent., the lowest being zero (address at the Jerusalem Conference), the highest being 100 per cent. (address to Sanhedrin before his imprisonment). Leaving these extremes, the percentage of ascriptives ranges from $33\frac{1}{3}$ to 75 per cent., and thus shows great variation.

Fourthly, the average of adverbials in all his addresses is $41\frac{2}{3}$, the lowest being zero (to the Sanhedrin before imprisonment), the highest being 100 (at Jerusalem Conference), while the rest of the Petrine addresses range fairly well about the general average ($41\frac{2}{3}$). Still the variations here are great.

Fifthly, in these addresses are no complementary participles, except in the short address to Simon Magus (only one participle, and that complementary in indirect discourse), and in the address to the apostles and the Jerusalem church, chap. 11, in which $41\frac{2}{3}$ per cent. of the participles are

73

complementary, the large percentage being due largely to the telling of the visions.

Can we from these facts arrive at any definite conclusion as to the composition of the Petrine addresses? Did the author of First Peter compose these addresses and the author of the Book of Acts reproduce them in his book? First Peter has an average of $15\frac{2}{3}$ participles per page, 55 per cent. ascriptive and 45 per cent. adverbial. The ratio between the ascriptives and adverbials is about the same in the Petrine addresses and in First Peter (55 to 45 in First Peter, $48\frac{1}{3}$ to $41\frac{2}{3}$ in the Petrine addresses). Of course, the presence of so many complementary participles in the Petrine addresses is largely due to the visions described, as is shown by the absence of any complementary participles from the most of the Petrine addresses. The style agrees fairly well with that of First Peter in which is not found one complementary participle. But, since it is not certain according to many New Testament scholars that Peter the apostle wrote First Peter, this comparison of the participial usage of the Petrine addresses and First Peter cannot bring us to any definite conclusion.

Again, let us compare the participial usage of the Petrine addresses with the first portion in which they are all (except one) imbedded. The average in chaps. 1-12 is $15\frac{1}{6}$, with $34\frac{7}{12}$ per cent. ascriptive, $57\frac{7}{8}$ per cent. adverbial, $ca.$ $7\frac{3}{4}$ per cent. complementary. The average for the Petrine addresses is $11\frac{4}{6}+$, with $48\frac{1}{3}$ per cent. ascriptive, $41\frac{2}{3}$ per cent. adverbial, 10 per cent. complementary. That is, the average in the addresses is over 3 per cent. lower than that in chaps. 1-12. This average is not necessarily against the free composition of the Petrine addresses by the author of the Book of Acts, because addresses usually have a lower average, even when written by the same author, than pure narrative.

But the ratio between the ascriptives and adverbials suggests a different conclusion. In the Petrine addresses the ratio is $48\frac{1}{3}$ to $41\frac{2}{3}$, while in the first portion it is $34\frac{7}{12}$ to $57\frac{7}{8}$. That is, the author in the addresses shows a Jewish-Greek style (the majority of the participles being ascriptive) while the Petrine portion approaches more nearly to the participial usage of a classical or κοινή writer. Yet, it is to be noted, from the table on p. 19, that the address from Solomon's Porch resembles more closely the later chapters, 13-28. Also the address to the apostles and Jerusalem church, chap. 11, has the participial tone of chaps. 13-28. Hence, we may conclude:

First, as to the number of participles, the composition of the Petrine addresses might be either that of the author of First Peter, or of the author of chaps. 1-12.

Secondly, as to the ratio between ascriptives and adverbials, the participial usage of the addresses is very different from that of chaps. 1–12, and so suggests that, if the author of the book did freely compose the Petrine addresses, he either assumed a Jewish-Greek style, or followed closely a Jewish-Christian source for the addresses.

SEC. 104.   COMPOSITION OF THE ADDRESSES OF GAMALIEL AND STEPHEN

The former (p. 19) averages only $2\frac{1}{2}$ participles per page, containing only one (adverbial) participle. This address seems to be a free composition of the author, yet the style is not strikingly that of the author, and surely the low average would suggest a Jewish composition (Gamaliel's).

The address of Stephen has the Jewish tone as to average ($11\frac{1}{10}$) but the ratio of ascriptives and adverbials, $34\frac{4}{5}$ to $59\frac{4}{5}$, resembles closely the style of chaps. 1–12. It is probable from these figures that the author had a Hellenistic-Christian written source, but worked it over somewhat to suit the purpose of his book.

SEC. 105.   THE COMPOSITION OF THE PAULINE ADDRESSES

We make the following observations from facts on pp. 19 and 20:

First, the average of all the Pauline addresses is ca. $17\frac{1}{2}$, the lowest being 9 (address to the ship's crew in the storm) and the highest (address to the Lystrans) being $25\frac{5}{7}$ per page. These are both short addresses. The longer addresses range fairly well about the general average.

Secondly, the average for ascriptives in the Pauline addresses is $39\frac{1}{2}$ per cent., the lowest being zero (address to Jews in Rome) and the highest 60 per cent. (address in Pisidian Antioch). The rest swing fairly well about the general average, except the address before Felix with $7\frac{9}{13}$ per cent. ascriptive and the address to the Athenians with 20 per cent. ascriptive.

Thirdly, the average of adverbials in the Pauline addresses is $54\frac{1}{2}$ per cent., the lowest being 40 per cent. (address in Pisidian Antioch) and the highest 100 per cent. (address to Jews in Rome). The percentage of the rest of the Pauline addresses swings in moderate proximity about their general average (except the address to the Athenians with its excessive 80 per cent. adverbials).

Fourthly, only three out of the nine Pauline addresses contain complementary participles, the lowest being $5\frac{5}{7}$ per cent., the highest $30\frac{10}{13}$, the other $30\frac{1}{3}$ per cent.

Fifthly, according to facts on p. 23, we observe that Paul's average in Galatians, I Corinthians, and Romans is ca. 9, with about three-fourths ascriptives, one-fourth adverbials, and scarcely any complementary participles.

Hence we conclude from these facts and observations:

First, the participial usage in the Pauline addresses is strongly non-Pauline—almost anti-Pauline.

Secondly, it is likely that the author of the Book of Acts freely worked over the matter of the Pauline addresses and thus left on them the stamp of his own style rather than that of Paul. In a few of these addresses (especially in that in Pisidian Antioch, that to the Ephesian elders, that to the Jewish people in Aramaic, and that to the Lystrans) the style has some Pauline marks, yet the participial usage in these addresses resembles too closely that of the author to be regarded as the actual composition of Paul reproduced by the author.

SEC. 106. THE COMPOSITION OF THE NON-CHRISTIAN ADDRESSES

These are by Demetrius to the workmen of Ephesus, by the town-clerk of Ephesus, by Tertullus against Paul, by Festus to Agrippa, and include also Lysias' letter to Felix. We have no other literary productions from these men with which to compare these addresses. See p. 20 for facts. We observe that the usage of the participle in these addresses is remarkably similar to that of chaps. 13–28, and this suggests their free composition by the author of the book.

BIBLIOGRAPHY

GREEK GRAMMARS

Winer-Moulton, *New Testament Grammar*. 1882. Based on G. B. Winer, *Grammatik des neutestamentlichen Sprachidioms*. 1822; 1855.

Hadley and Allen, *Greek Grammar*. 1884; 1889.

Goodwin, *Moods and Tenses*. 1860; 1890.

Kuehner, *Griechische Grammatik*. 1890.

Monro, *A Grammar of the Homeric Dialect*. 1891.

Burton, *Syntax of the Moods and Tenses in New Testament Greek*. 1893; fifth ed., 1903.

Jannaris, *Historical Greek Grammar*. 1897.

Babbitt, *Greek Grammar*. 1902.

John Thompson, *A Greek Grammar*. 1902.

Buttmann, *Grammatik des neutestamentlichen Sprachidioms*. 1859.

Blass, *Grammatik des neutestamentlichen Griechisch*. 1896. Zweite Auflage, 1902.

Brugmann-Delbrück, *Vergleichende Syntax der indogermanischen Sprachen*. Zweiter Theil. Strassburg, 1897.

Winer-Schmiedel, *Winers Grammatik des neutestamentlichen Sprachidioms*. 8. Auflage. 1894-.

Viteau, *Syntaxe des Propositions*. 1893.

Viteau, *Etude sur le Grec du Nouveau Testament*. 1896.

J. H. Moulton, *Grammar of New Testament Greek*, Vol. I, Prolegomena. 1906.

WORKS OF INTRODUCTION ON ACTS

Bleek, *Einleitung in das Neue Testament*. 1862. 2. Aufl., 1870. 4. Aufl., 1886.

Hilgenfeld, *Einleitung in das Neue Testament*. 1875.

Holtzmann, *Einleitung in das Neue Testament*. 1885. 3. Aufl., 1892.

B. Weiss, *Einleitung in das Neue Testament*. 1889. Dritte Aufl., 1897.

Zahn, *Einleitung in das Neue Testament*. 1897. Zweite Aufl., 1900.

Davidson, *Introduction to the New Testament*. 1882.

Reuss, *Geschichte der heiligen Schriften des Neuen Testamentes*. 1842. 6. Aufl., 1887.

Salmon, *Introduction to the New Testament*. 1892. 9th ed., 1899.

Bacon, *Introduction to the New Testament*. 1900.

Juelicher, *Einleitung in das Neue Testament*. 1894. 5. and 6. Aufl., 1906.

COMMENTARIES AND HISTORIES OF THE APOSTOLIC AGE

H. Holtzmann, *Die Apostolgeschichte im Hand-Commentar zum Neuen Testament*. 1889. Dritte Aufl., 1901.

Rackham, *Commentary on Acts*. 1901.

Wendt, *Apostelgeschichte*, Meyer Kommentar. 8. Aufl., 1899.

77

Weizsäcker, *Das apostolische Zeitalter der christlichen Kirche.* 1886. 3. Aufl., 1902.
McGiffert, *A History of the Apostolic Age.* 1897.
Bartlet, *The Apostolic Age.* 1899.
Ropes, *The Apostolic Age.* 1906.

MISCELLANEOUS

Harnack, *Die Chronologie der altchristlichen Litteratur bis Eusebius (Geschichte der altchrist. Lit.,* II, I). 1897.
Harnack, *Lukas der Arzt der Verfasser des dritten Evangeliums und Apostelgeschichte.* 1906.
Harnack, *Die Apostelgeschichte.* 1908.
C. Clemen, *Die Chronologie der Paulinischen Briefe.* 1893.
J. Weiss, *Ueber die Absicht und der literarische Charakter der Apostelgeschichte.* 1897.
Spitta, *Apostelgeschichte.* 1891.
Bethge, *Die Paulinischen Reden der Apostelgeschichte.* 1887.
Dalman, *Die Worte Jesu.* 1898.
Lekebusch, *Die Composition und Entstehung der Apostelgeschichte.* 1854.
Deissmann, *Bibelstudien,* 1895; *Neue Bibelstudien,* 1897.
Deissmann, *New Lights on Biblical Greek.* 1908.
Thumb, *Die griechische Sprache im Zeitalter des Hellenismus,* chap. v. 1901.
Kretschmer, *Die Entstehung der Koiné.* 1900.
Krenkel, *Josephus und Lucas.* 1894.
Ramsay, *St. Paul the Traveler.* 1896.
Ramsay, *The Church in the Roman Empire.* 1894.
Ramsay, *Pauline and Other Studies,* etc. 1907.
Chase, *The Credibility of the Book of the Acts of the Apostles.* 1902.
Plummer, *Commentary on Luke* ("International Critical Commentary"). 1896. Introduction, §6.
Hawkins, *Horae Synopticae,* pp. 148–54. 1899.
Burkitt, F. C., *The Gospel History and Its Transmission,* chap. iv. 1906.
Simcox, *Language of the New Testament,* pp. 122–34. 1890.
Hobart, *Medical Language in St. Luke.* 1882.
Hatch, *Essays in Biblical Greek.* 1889.
Kennedy, *Sources of New Testament Greek.* 1895.
Hastings, *Dictionary of the Bible,* art. "Acts" (Headlam); "Language of the New Testament" (Thayer).
Encyclopedia Biblica, art. "Acts" (Schmiedel).

MAGAZINE ARTICLES

Theologische Rundschau, 1897–98, pp. 371; 1900, pp. 50 f.; 1901, pp. 66 f.; 1903, pp. 79 f.; 1904, pp. 278 f. (C. Clemen reviews literature on *Apostelge-*

schichte); 1899, pp. 47 f., 83 f., 129 f. (H. Heitmüller reviews literature on *Die Quellenfrage in der Apostelgeschichte*); 1902, pp. 58 f. (Deissmann, *Die Sprache der griechischen Bibel*); April, 1907 (C. Clemen replies to Harnack on Lukas der Arzt).

Zeitschrift für wissenschaftliche Theologie, 1895, pp. 65 f., 186 f., 384 f., 481 f.; 1896, pp. 24 f., 177 f., 351 f., 517 f. (a series of eight articles by Hilgenfeld on *Die Apostelgeschichte nach ihren Quellen-Schrifte untersucht*).

Theologische Literaturzeitung, 1906, p. 466 (Harnack replies to Schürer on "Lukas der Arzt").

Zeitschrift für protestantische Theologie, 1890 (Feine, "Die alte Quelle in der ersten Hälfte der Apostelgeschichte").

Theologische Studien und Kritiken, 1873 (Kähler, "Die Reden des Petrus in der Apostelgeschichte").

Classical Review, XV, 31–38, 434–42; XVIII, 106–12, 151–55 (J. H. Moulton, "Grammatical Notes from the Papyri").

American Journal of Philology, I, 45 f. (Gildersleeve, Encroachments of μή on οὐ in Later Greek"); IV, 291 f. (W. J. Alexander, "Participial Periphrases in Attic Prose"); VI, 310 f. (Spieker, "Genitive Absolute in Attic Orators"); IX, 137 f. (Gildersleeve, "On the Stylistic Effect of the Greek Participle").

Transactions of the American Philological Association, IV, 45 f. (W. A. Stevens, "The Substantive Use of the Greek Participle"); XII, 88 f. (T. D. Seymour, "The Use of the Greek Aorist Participle").

American Journal of Theology, July, 1907 ("Bacon on Acts vs. Galatians").

Biblical World, I, pp. 163 f. (editorial on "N. T. Grammar"); VI, 39 f. (Burton on "The Book of Acts"); X, 350 f. (Mathews reviews McGiffert's *Apostolic Age*); XVII, 355 f. (Bumstead, "Acts: the Present State of Criticism"); XIX, 190 f. (J. H. Moulton, "New Lights on Biblical Greek"); XIX, 238 f. (Review of Warfield's *Speeches in Acts in Bible Student*, January, 1902); XIX, 268 f. (Bartlet, "The Character and Composition of Acts"); XIX, 414 f., 423 f. (Editorial, "Notes and Comments on Portions of Acts"); XX, 260 f., 370 f. (Knowling, "The Medical Language of St. Luke"); XXII, 3 f. (Editorial on "The Lucan Writings").

The Expositor, fifth series, Vol. I, 129 f., 212 f. (Ramsay reviews Blass on the two editions of Acts); Vol. VII, 1 f. (Ramsay on "The Authorship of Acts"); sixth series, Vol. III, 271 f., Vol. VII, 104 f., Vol. VIII, 423 f. (J. H. Moulton, "Notes from the Papyri"); seventh series, Vol. II, 481 f., Vol. III, 97 f. (Ramsay reviews Harnack's *Luke the Physician*, etc.); Vol. IV, 289 f. (Deissmann, "The Philology of the Greek Bible").

The Expository Times, Vol. VIII, 166 f. (Tasker reviews Zöckler on "The Recent Criticism of Acts"); Vol. IX, 272 f. (Banks reviews Deissmann's *Bibelstudien and Neue Bibelstudien*); XVII, 450 f. (Kennedy reviews Moulton's *Prolegomena*).

In addition to the above the following texts have been used: Wescott and Hort, *The New Testament in Greek*, the texts and editions mentioned in the treatise for Homer, Sophocles, Herodotus, Xenophon, Thucydides, Demosthenes, Plato, Polybius, Strabo, the Septuagint (including Second Maccabees), Josephus, Plutarch, and Tischendorf, *Novum Testamentum Graece*, Octava Editio.

www.ingramcontent.com/pod-product-compliance
Lightning Source LLC
LaVergne TN
LVHW051705080426
835511LV00017B/2737